Fragment

Fragments of an Infinite Memory

My Life with the Internet

MAËL RENOUARD

Translated from the French by Peter Behrman de Sinéty

 New York Review Books New York

This is a New York Review Book
published by The New York Review of Books
435 Hudson Street, New York, NY 10014
www.nyrb.com

Copyright © 2016 by Éditions Grasset & Fasquelle
Translation copyright © 2021 by Peter Behrman de Sinéty
All rights reserved.

Library of Congress Cataloging-in-Publication Data
Names: Renouard, Maël, author. | Behrman de Sinéty, Peter, translator.
Title: Fragments of an infinite memory : my life with the internet /
    by Maël Renouard / translated by Peter Behrman de Sinéty.
Other titles: Fragments d'une mémoire infinie. English
Description: New York : New York Review Books, [2020] |
Identifiers: LCCN 2019025144 (print) | LCCN 2019025145 (ebook) | ISBN
    9781681372808 (trade paperback) | ISBN 9781681372815 (ebook)
Subjects: LCSH: Renouard, Maël—Notebooks, sketchbooks, etc. | Internet.
Classification: LCC PQ2718.E57 F7313 2016 (print) |
    LCC PQ2718.E57 (ebook) | DDC 848/.9203—dc23
LC record available at https://lccn.loc.gov/2019025144
LC ebook record available at https://lccn.loc.gov/2019025145

ISBN 978-1-68137-280-8
Available as an electronic book; ISBN 978-1-68137-281-5

Printed in the United States of America on acid-free paper.

1 2 3 4 5 6 7 8 9 10

Fragments of an Infinite Memory

1

ONE DAY, AS I was daydreaming on the boulevard Beaumarchais, I had the idea—it came and went in a flash, almost in spite of myself—of Googling to find out what I'd been up to and where I'd been two evenings before, at five o'clock, since I couldn't remember on my own. This must have been in November or December 2008; I remember the intersection near the Cirque d'Hiver where I was standing, about to cross the street, the light of that cold, gray afternoon, and the spark that shot through my mind.

It wasn't simply a matter of retrieving the information as from some mysterious guardian angel, snitch, or record keeper, the way a citizen of East Germany could have consulted his file at the secret police archives, an odd enough thought. The moment of which I'm speaking offered something else: a vision of the present instant already transformed into its digital image, slowed down, blurred, wobbly, like a video on YouTube.

Images like that were no longer imperfect traces of past moments, miraculously captured. Instead the world had embodied the mode of being of those kinds of images, and I could see it quietly uniting with an infinite stock of videos from which we would later be able to extract the image of every past instant. We can already do this with recorded images, but my daydream was that the distinction between recorded and unrecorded moments had vanished. No technology was required for the world to preserve itself in its entirety. In that instant of disarray, I had fleetingly perceived this transition toward a new mode of being—this becoming-image-memory, so to speak—and web portals had become simply the wells from which we could draw a few of the innumerable images in which the entirety of the world's past could be retrieved. Technology no longer served to record: it gave access to Being's own recording of itself.

•

Claude Lévi-Strauss says somewhere that even two or three minutes of film recorded by a camera placed in the streets of Pericles's Athens would be enough to overturn our entire historiography of antiquity.

According to my dream, a person could, with a little patience, locate in the recesses of YouTube those three minutes of sun, dust, palaver, Logos so thick you could cut it with a knife.

•

"A great video = a glimpse into the past," someone once noted in the comments to a YouTube excerpt from *The Threepenny Opera*, probably the film version directed by G. W. Pabst in 1931. This was some years ago, in 2008 or 2009; would it be possible to retrieve the comment today? The excerpt must have been "Die Moritat von Mackie Messer," a piece I was listening to then—and watching—in every available performance. I remember one of my favorites was a Czech-language version dating back to the 1950s or 1960s.

•

In 1956, Edgar Morin wrote in *The Cinema, or The Imaginary Man*: "Numerous science fiction stories have as their subject the *cinematographic recovery of time*, to the point of recapturing an incorruptible fragment of the past. Élie Faure develops an analogous vision when he imagines the inhabitants of a distant planet, living at the time of the crucifixion of Jesus, sending us by missile a film that would make us actual witnesses."

There is an old daydream that locates the storeroom of the past in distant space. Canto 34 of *Orlando Furioso* describes the moon as the locus of time regained. All things that have vanished from the Earth are gathered there—lovers' tears and sighs, time spent idly gambling, unfinished projects, unquenched desires, the glory of past kings and of empires stricken from the map. A rich daydream that has since been revived by science fiction: the touching thing about *Close Encounters of the Third Kind* is the idea that the aviators who vanish from the Bermuda Triangle have gone elsewhere, under the care of angelic aliens whose barely glimpsed profiles essentially represent a victory over time. As if the loss of those dear to us was never absolute—as if they might be kept somewhere in reserve, waiting for and awaited by us, as if this disappearance was the price to pay for a salvation that makes final reunions always possible.

•

Where is the past? Henri Bergson dismisses this question at the same time he poses it, by saying that the past is, precisely, not stored anywhere but rather persists in itself, entire, in its own mode of being, in a virtual state. The past is "pure memory," which we cannot access as such; for the work of memory is always, according to Bergson, a reactualization of this virtual past through images (on this point, Gilles Deleuze will attempt to go beyond Bergson, by positing a direct perception of the virtual). In my boulevard Beaumarchais daydream, it seemed to me that the world—in relation to its infinite past—had become capable of doing what each consciousness can do in relation to its subjective life: delve into the past to retrieve images. In this world consciousness, YouTube videos had become the image-memories that reactualize the virtual past which has slipped from our grasp, a virtual past which has ceased to be present, but has not ceased to be.

•

Georges Charpak had an intuition that comes very close to my dream of a self-recording, retrospectively accessible Being when he wondered if it might be possible to retrieve sounds and voices from the past, unintentionally recorded on artifacts whose making involved tracing grooves: like vinyl records before their time. He was thinking of pottery in particular. He walked the halls of the Louvre in search of Greek or Mesopotamian objects that might lend themselves to such a study, though in the end he gave up on it. The chance of success, he figured, was too slim to justify the funds it would require.

•

Candidates for the École Normale Supérieure, *khâgneux*, were traditionally expected to accumulate an immense amount of knowledge. As a diversion, they would invent exam questions that were altogether unfathomable and eccentric:

"Who extinguished what?"

"Théodose extinguished the sacred flame, in AD 391."

The internet is an infallible intellect, its knowledge no longer a ridiculous extract from the infinite space of past events, and now if you type "Who extinguished what?" into Google, you will find the answer: it appears on the website of the Académie Française, in Marcel Achard's speech welcoming Thierry Maulnier, where he invokes a passage from Robert Brasillach's memoirs recounting that Maulnier was famous at the Lycée Louis-le-Grand for being able to reply to baroque questions like that. He could even tell you what happened next.

•

From simple riddles to the divinatory power the Greeks attributed to enigmas is not so large a step. The automatic production of results, even for questions that strictly preclude an answer, yields oblique paths, in the manner of the old oracles.

The ancients sought to read the future in the figures formed by stones or die cast upon the ground. For some people, to throw a few words into Google has become a new form of divination— *googlemancy*.

•

A., unacquainted with Lenin's work, one day Googled: "What is to be done?" The answer came up right away: revolution.

7

•

One evening, P. told me a story from 2007 or 2008, when the craze for Facebook was quickly spreading. As a teenager, he had secretly been in love with M. de L., a girl he met one summer at a sailing club on coast of the Vendée, only to lose sight of her when the vacation was over. She was from Versailles; he was from a large town in the provinces. For a few months, he was haunted by her memory, but by the time he finished lycée and moved to Paris, the torment was long forgotten. One day, fifteen years after that summer in the Vendée, he found M. among the Facebook "friends" of one of his own friends in Paris, T., whom he had met much later and only after various coincidences and sheer luck had carried him infinitely far from his life as a teenager. He realized that this friend—whom he had also sailed with when they were about twenty-five, before Facebook existed—had to be the boy M. had mentioned going catamaraning with in Corsica earlier in the summer of 1993 when he had met her. T. was from Corsica. The ages matched. P.'s memory could no longer firmly establish whether T. was the name M. had mentioned to him, but he persuaded himself it was. There was no doubting it. In any case, he was careful not to risk proving it false by being too curious. Since his love had entirely faded, P. let things be; he did nothing. He was pleased, though, to experience a new kind of dramatic device that hadn't yet figured in any plot—a recognition scene unaccounted for in Aristotle's *Poetics*. He felt he was at the heart of a story the possibility of which had arisen at the very moment the story began. The sensation was all the more striking in that he saw himself as a character in a story, and at the same time he had the impression of finding, within his own being, the standpoint of an

8

omniscient narrator playfully interweaving the strands of several lives. One of the charms of Proust's *In Search of Lost Time* lies in this sort of connection—revealed on the plane of time regained—between people who at first glance seem to belong to completely divergent walks of life. On the internet, P. found in his own existence an unexpected approximation to Proust's time regained, that restoration all our lives contain in part, though it always remains notional, since in Proust it only takes place thanks to two unique circumstances: the unrealistic knowledge of the thoughts and destinies of others that his narrator possesses (he is, precisely, both a character and an omniscient narrator), and the peculiar limits of the aristocratic world, whose members, with more or less insincerity, are always exclaiming, "What a small world it is!"—and so it is, because they keep running into their cousins. The expression "it's a small world" is telling enough, but it is of limited application when it comes to the internet. Just because you can explore a vast world doesn't mean that it's small. On the contrary, exploration is what allows this infinity to define and unfurl itself. Leibniz hits the mark here: the more connections a world contains, the more infinite it is.

•

Who hasn't gone on the internet looking for past loves and friends not seen for years? Time lost in search of lost time.

•

David Lodge published *Small World* in 1984. This "small world" isn't merely that of an internationalized academia where scholars—

without borders, but strictly among initiates—debate the merits of structuralism, deconstruction, and old-fashioned literary history. It's a world linked by telephones and traversed by jet planes. Morris Zapp, one of the novel's main characters, arrives at a theory of sorts that he says applies only to scholars, but that is not the case. "There are," he says, "three things which have revolutionized academic life in the last twenty years, though very few people have woken up to the fact: jet travel, direct-dialing phones, and the Xerox." In light of these innovations, material coexistence in a single place is no longer necessary for collaborative work and information-sharing. According to Zapp's prophecy, which hasn't exactly come to pass, it would soon matter less and less whether you belonged to Harvard University or to the University of Rummidge (Rummidge being a provincial English town invented by Lodge, endowed at the end of the sixties with an institution of higher education that ages quickly and poorly), since a scholar would only have to travel from conference to conference, photocopies in hand, to participate in a kind of "global campus."

Zapp's predictions sound like the ones made some ten or fifteen years later, when internet use first became widespread. But there are some significant differences. David Lodge's world still leaves room for loss, for disappearance, for the difficulty of reunions, for desperate searching. This only heightens the irony that Lodge injects into the predictions of Zapp—a kind of demagogic and brilliant academic whose talents dance a little upon thin air, whose affable verve is at once amusing and heavy-handed, and who, in spite of his rather naive boasting, is never entirely unlikable. The novel tells the story of a young literary scholar, Persse McGarrigle, who amorously pursues a young woman he met at a conference. He constantly wonders where she is. He no sooner picks up her trail than she is already elsewhere. It does him little good to have all the jet planes he could possibly hope for; his agony is the same as that of the lover in the Song of Songs when she asks the daughters of Jerusalem if any of them has seen her beloved. An unlimited increase in the physical possibility of locomotion is far different from access to the information that can usefully guide locomotion: our capacity for locomotion is indeed considerable in relation to what it was in prior centuries, but it remains blind and absurd if left to its own devices.

Lodge's world is still an exhausting world. A world in which it is possible to run in vain. A world in which a person can disappear forever. A world in which you always have to hope for the grace of coincidences. Lodge multiplies such coincidences wittingly and abundantly. They are part of a network of allusions that link his novel to traditional narrative forms, at times picaresque, at times Arthurian. The world of literature itself turns out to be a small world, a world of winks between old friends. This ironically seems to indicate that despite all the pompous prophecies spurred on by technological progress, things perhaps haven't changed so much since the times of Perceval or Lazarillo de Tormes, when, at least in stories, the marvelous and the extravagant would come to strengthen the weak human hold on a world too big for its grasp, too exposed to forgetfulness and destruction. If the phrase *small world* means anything, it doubtless means something far different from what Zapp imagines. No matter how convincingly we represent Heathrow Airport as one of the central crossroads of a global village, the young hero is still in danger of finding nothing there but helplessness, errancy, and despair in the face of an infinite number of possible directions. And he would indeed find just that, if it weren't for the miraculous and kindly intervention of the airline company employee Cheryl Summerbee, a kind of good fairy (holding Spenser's *The Faerie Queene* in her hands) who attracts good fortune and knows how to spread it around.

When it comes to forgetfulness and disorientation, it's natural to feel that Google and GPS have changed the nature of our experience far more profoundly than the jumbo jet and the photocopier. There is something particularly striking about the way a new smartphone can fill the gaps in our memory or knowledge for nearly every factual question liable to cross our minds (What time is the next ferry? Who was the French prime minister in 1955?); just as the same smartphone can show us, on a map whose scale varies infinitely at the touch of a finger, where we are on Earth and what is this dusty path through the open countryside on which we have just set foot. And a world in which Persse McGarrigle can type "Angelica Pabst" into Google, or find his way to her on Facebook through likely mutual acquaintances, is no longer a world in which only the charmed luck of novels could rescue his amorous quest.

•

We might want to reconsider what we make of the coming of the internet as well. After all, there are still people whose traces on Google are infinitesimal or nonexistent, and many things remain insufficiently archived. Or we could point out that, in fact, it has been a long time since the phone book first allowed one to look up a name, and even longer since sextant and compass considerably reduced human disorientation in uncharted or unmarked zones.

Each generation sees the technological advances of the previous era—no matter how near—as excrescences of an ancient world. People like to think the world has only truly changed in their own time. But the feeling of witnessing a spectacular acceleration that rejects outright all past centuries, relegating them to an undifferentiated backwater incommensurable with current experience, is not solely the privilege of children who grew up with the internet and see the gigantic computers conceived after World War II as antiques no less foreign to contemporary life than the powdered wigs of the 1700s or the quadrigae of the Circus Maximus. "That the world has never changed so much in a single century (except by destruction) is a fact with which we are all familiar. I myself have seen the sparrows swooping down on the horse-drawn buses at the Palais Royal—and the shy and charming Colonel Glenn on his return from the cosmos," wrote Malraux in 1965. But a person who, before Malraux's birth, had seen the emergence of cinema and aviation might legitimately have had the same feeling of witnessing a fundamental upheaval in human history. It would not have been baseless, for that matter, to tell the younger generations that Neil Armstrong's exploits were essentially offshoots of Clément Ader's or the Wright brothers'. And a person who, even a little earlier, had beheld the first daguerreotypes could in turn have claimed that *he* was the one who had witnessed the veritable revolution, of which cinema had merely developed the consequences. Against the grain of that enthusiasm which sees the present moment as the most radical, the most historically significant, we would need to slide further and further into the past, the cursor marking the authentic breakthrough, until we found the event that, more humble perhaps in appearance than the subsequent innovations, nevertheless constituted their necessary condition: the invention that truly broke new ground, that truly changed the face of the Earth, because it sprang forth unplanned, unawaited, unforeseen. Who's right? Who's more naive?

The theory of exponentially increasing change has the merit of lending credence to these ever more frequent proclamations of revolution. It posits an actual acceleration of technological progress at the root of our—prideful and naive, but also pertinent—feeling that upheavals in human history have become nearly daily occurrences. While people prudently used to wait centuries before uttering "Never till this day," we seem to have gradually authorized ourselves to say this every few decades, then every few years, soon perhaps every few months. The hopes that Raymond Kurzweil draws from this theory, of which he is a proponent, are controversial. They cast doubt upon his objectivity, for they seem less a possible consequence of his calculations than the expression of a fundamental dream which these calculations appear miraculously to deliver: the promise of witnessing the approach, and perhaps even the achievement, of immortality.

•

What creates the revolutionary feeling of these successive advances— what makes them seem incommensurable with their antecedents—is perhaps the feeling that through them a certain *telos* is taking on clearer and clearer form (and even, in a sense, revealing itself at last as *telos*), much as each step becomes ever more exhilarating for a runner approaching the finish line, even though his steps have not changed.

The current state of our technological advances has given us the internet's infinite stock of information at our fingertips, along with our exact position on a map of the Earth, thanks to a device that fits in our pocket. The daydreams that shape these technological advances can easily be projected into the future.

The body barrier will be broken. Our mental life will directly annex these auxiliaries which at the moment are still exterior to it. They will enter the inner depths of the mind. The increasing convergence of the biological and the electronic—which lies at the core of nanotechnology—affords a clearer and clearer glimpse of this possibility.

We will do a Google search exactly as we go looking through our memories, by a simple act of the mind which, like memory, will require neither the hand nor the eye as intermediary. We will use this inner Google to look up words and phrases in a foreign language. We will know the name of the tree, the history of the public monument, the biography of Casimir Delavigne, as soon as our sight data is recorded and processed. And this is not all, by any means. Each thing will deploy itself beneath our gaze in its monadic singularity, that is, in the infinity of its nature, its history, its relations to the entire world. The memory of which our brain is the organ will no longer be an individual memory.

Deleuze was struck by how Bergson said in *Matter and Memory* that we plunge into the virtual past in order to find our memories there and bring them to the surface of consciousness, as upon the surface of the ocean. The internet has given an outward form to this process. One day, it will return to the inwardness from which it came.

•

The interiorization of *hypomnemata*—memory props, such as writing—is not necessarily a victorious return of "presence" and an objection to the Derridean theory of *différance*.

Derrida's theory deconstructs both the metaphysical aspiration

15

toward pure self-presence and the oppositions upon which it rests: origin/derivation; source/supplement; signification/trace; soul/extension; intellect/sense; speech/writing. His theory shows that no term is ever primary or secondary, but that the two terms of an opposition are always already intimately connected. Derrida spoke of "*arche*-writing" to indicate that, even in the absence of the written word, thought is intrinsically made of a movement of exteriorization, extension, detachment, differentiation: this movement is the transcendental condition of the written word, which in turn bears witness to and phenomenonalizes this movement.

The internet exhibits precisely such an inner extension of the mind. That's why it naturally gives rise to the dream that the mind is inhabitable, that you could wander around in it, take refuge, and find salvation there.

·

The final stage of this inward extension of the mind would be the ontological equation of inner and outer, with all its practical consequences: the mental appropriation of the world, the upthrust of a world born of our daydreams.

·

This would be, according to Bruce Benderson, the end of imagination achieved by the victory of imagination.

·

A lessening of the difference between inner and outer has already largely begun. The internet is a space in which to explore everything that crosses our minds—curiosity, worry, fantasy. Hence the ethical questions that were born along with it. Plato condemned the tyrant as someone who has the possibility of enacting his darkest passions —of actually living his dreams which should have remained the only theater of those passions, in the secret recesses of sleep. Morality is what stands in opposition to the dream of exposing others absolutely to our passions.

•

Two fundamental tendencies, distinct but easily linked, orient the increase in our technical capacity to travel and to archive: the possibility of leaving the Earth, and the possibility of taking everything on Earth along with us.

Consider, for example, the nearly simultaneous invention of the airplane and the motion-picture camera. It is tempting—but all the more risky, as the time scale shrinks even more—to look for other conjunctions: Sputnik and the first hard drive; the first moon steps and the first microprocessor.

This parallel development is latent in the workings of the mind rather than a matter of premeditation, and yet it would appear to be quite impossible to formulate a law that would explain such coincidences.

In fact, the two tendencies can clash. Over the past few years, the flow and storage of digital information for domestic use has increased far more rapidly than our capacity for space travel. If there were a reliable law, the first USB stick or the first smartphone would surely have coincided at least with a voyage to Mars.

The spirit of the times is not solely to blame. What's the good of physically leaving Earth, when the world is entering deeper and deeper into the dimension of mind, and when we in turn—to our ruin or salvation—are plunging into this inner, immaterial infinity. Teilhard de Chardin expressed this overlapping of two tendencies. He wrote: "I imagine our noosphere is destined to shut in solitude upon itself—and it is not in a spatial but rather in a mental direction that we shall find our line of escape, without having to leave or even extend beyond the Earth." For Teilhard de Chardin, the accomplished mind, detached from its material matrix, attains this faculty of resting upon itself in what he calls the Omega Point. Perhaps at that point we will inhabit the infinite number of images we will have produced in the meantime. Some people speculate that, in a distant future, a megacomputer may serve as the medium from which this autonomous mental reality will emanate, sheltered from the comings and goings of matter.

•

Survival is not the only thing at stake in a victory of mind. The prize is also the ecstasy that would spring from dwelling in the realm of essences. Plato entrusted this hope to what would later be termed metaphysics. Romanticism left it to art.

Recollection supposes an identification of past and essence. For the loss of existence appears to reduce a thing to its essence, draws it into the dimension of pure and simple mind, a promise of final intelligibility. This is the root of the emotion produced by every memory and image of the past.

The Hegelian notion of *Erinnerung* describes the mind's access to what time has forced beyond the living present, the birth of the concept, which is the counterpart to death. Derrida once proposed to translate *Erinnerung* as "interiorizing memory" or even "intimation," since Hegel, by occasionally writing *Er-Innerung*, insists upon the interiorization inherent to this process of memory that summons things to mind.

Mind's appropriation of Being supposes, for Hegel, that the share accorded to matter, to images, to representation in general, be further and further diminished. That's why his *Aesthetics* establishes a hierarchy of the arts according to how at home the mind finds itself there, the degree of its separation from an exterior medium that only exhibits it in so far as it limits it. Poetry is more spiritual than painting, which is more spiritual than sculpture.

Memory technologies in part fulfill the Hegelian program, and in part contradict it. The realm of intimation doesn't grow larger as images decrease, but rather through their indefinite multiplication. Images are intimation. They have entered the sphere of mind. Just beyond this, they project the threshold of the Parousia of meaning, which never takes place. As interiorizations, images create the sense of an imminent revelation; as images, they never get beyond this promise, which isn't kept. To convert Being into information is not to reveal its meaning—no matter how close this conversion might approach to totality. *Erinnerung* happens, but there is a split. Meaning and memory part ways at the very moment when they seem about to collide. Then ecstasy comes forth as melancholy.

•

When, in the dead of night, we go searching on YouTube for the music of ten, twenty, or thirty years ago, we find that we have joined a community of lonely individuals leaving the trace of an intense, ambiguous feeling, born of a reunion with time past that can take place only because these moments have first been utterly lost: "This brings back so many memories," "*Es waren Zeiten*," "Why gone so fast".... The internet shows that recollection has charted the path of technology—infinite distancing and preservation—and melancholy is the future of emotion.

2

INTERNET = "My metal throat can speak all languages" + "I have more memories than if I'd lived a thousand years."

•

Graffiti found on the walls of YouTube. 2012–2014. Comments left below the videos of hits from the 1970s, 1980s, 1990s, 2000s. Spelling has been largely preserved.

End of the night in the Hacienda 88-89. Booming, through the smoke, strobes, oil wheels and projections. Joy and sadness —Que saudades da época que esse clipe me lembra —Tanti ma tanti ricordi con questo pezzo… —This song brings me so many memories— Recordar —Ah woww! quels beaux souvenirs! —Anyone else on Nostalgia train? —Yeah I don't know if I enjoy this song or cry — Träume sind vorbei doch die Musik bleibt —I'm feeling old suddenly —While listening this song I have tears in my eyes —Been looking for this for a long time —Every time I listen to old skool classics I always think deep about my past and how fast the time has gone since the early 90's, the atmosphere back then was just different hard to explain but I think u all know what I'm getting at. —What would I give to relieve these times… —I felt my reincarnation

23

—I distinctly remember driving down Scrubs Lane some time in the summer of 2001, after 9 pm, listening to Capital FM when this came on. It was pouring outside in a tropical rain, some of the best moments of my life... —Bring old good memories <3—Warm breeze days, sitting by the park listening to this while I wait to play a game of basketball. Ahh good old days —Endlich wiedergefunden, suche den Song seit Jahrzehnten —Enfim... que nostalgia... puxa... —Ja, ich auch erinnere es auf Italienisch MTV um November-Dezember von 2000 —I adore this. Must be the memories. —Ich es für ein lange her diskogänger ein feines OLDSCHOOL Lied ich fand klasse gleich mal chill out —Takes me back, sick beat — Catorce años despues, esta cancion aun pega con todo! —Oh my, oh my, those memories! —This song always makes me feel like I'm just chilling far away on a beach, just warmth, sun and fun —90's were so great that we didn't notice when they left... and now we're missing them so much!!! —Nostalgia all over the place. —Trop de bons souvenirs de cette bonne époque... —This tune brings smile on my face even when I'm down. It's like a picture of the best memories from the craziest and happiest time in my life. Such a simple thing... such a great feeling :-) Thx3 —Saudades —Dose were the dayzzz B-)) —This song spoken recalls for me the memories of Christmas at Paris in the early 80's. Some streets were decorated with giant disco balls. Glitter ! —mùsicas dos meu tempo, che saudade desse tempo —Always great to hear this song. Thanks for the upload, and the memories that come with it! —Trop cool ce morceau la nostalgie —How time flies —Nostalgia brought me here. — Dudes, memories of my youth brought me here... —Rivoglio gli anni '80. Ecco. Adesso compro lo Yamaha dx-70 e faccio i Duran Duran. —Από την υπέροχη εποχή των *discothèque* —Υπέροχα τραγουδια μιας άλλης "φανταστικής" εποχής!!!!! —This brings time flooding back…so long ago. —Wahoooo cette musique me fait revenir en arriere —BLAST FROM THE PAST! —J'adore cette chanson souvenir de jeunesse, très belle époque…—Mc trae agradables recuerdos de los 80's —Santorini island 1985 greece hellas —Q musicaza…!!! Recuerdo tus labios, tus besos, y tus caricias, y sobre todo tu amor…:-) Siempre en mi corazon…Te amare siempre y estaras en un ladito de mi vida y seras unos de mis mas bellos recuerdos…:-(…—RIP Patrick —song brings back so many memories, thank you —I miss the good old times —This reminds me so much of partying in South Beach…fucked up off the ass…rollin balls… fuck…those were the days man for real! —Damn, I miss those days., —Wow so this must of been the hit back when bueller came out. Hop in a white camaro and put the roof down with a hot girl with crazy hair beside you. Livin the dream in 86' to this song — This was clubbing music. Z Cavaricci zuit suits chasing Madana look-a-likes and the Camaro was IROC…was a very good year —New Order always takes me back to my club days…funny how a song can trigger so many memories. —80's Flashback Cafe —Saudades Ilha de Capri festas boas —Brings you back to those late urban nights. No internet. No cell phones. Dennys or some all night Greek diner at pre dawn. —This song brought back many memories that shall remain hidden, ty music for being amazing and a pain in the ass at times —This song brings me memories I don't have —nostalgia di un passato che non ho mai vissuto —música del recuerdo ya que no la puedo olvidar a mi hermano le gusta esta música también —Oh to relive 1978 once again —Oh hell yah…I would sell my soul to the devil to relive those nites at the clubs…—We had 3 discos thurs sat sun nights was amazing laser shows met the girl of dreams

I remember sat in her house thinking is this happening donna summers mcarthur park was just released stunning song —Takes me back to 1979 in Germany in the Army Disco was everywhere —Sooo viele Erinnerungen! —I remember dancing to this at "The Saint" in lower Manhattan. Great club, non stop dancing, and my skirt was light green and so short. —Music time machine 1978 —#waybackmachine —Oh, sigh, those memories from the "era." —Damn! Everyone is having a nostalgia moment here. —The nostalgia is so deep on this one all I can do is well up inside and remember all the good times. Time stands still for nobody, but tracks like this sure are a welcoming window to yester year! —This takes me back to my undergrad years at Guelph —Been looking for it for ages, finally found it! —Great times that'll never come back. —In 2000 I was in Rosarito, Mexico, and I was too young to party, so I was trying to sleep, and this club outside was playing this song on repeat all night long and basically it has been stuck in my head for 14 years ponder that for a sec hard life made me this way —How many people think of a loved one lost when they hear this??? —Die erste Fahrt im VR6…der erste Cuba Libre…die durchgefeierten Nächte… —I was transported to 1995, wow wow epic… —know all of these songs…sorry to be cliche, but they are bringing back memories. —Das waren noch Zeiten —Time warp —now I'm travelling down memory lane —recordar viejos tempos —miércoles de recuerdo!! —momento nostalgia —I miss da 90's; (we need time travel…now!!!!! —Vaya temazooooo!!!!!! Que tiemposs buenos con este temaaaa!!!! —En is 2014 elke seconde… —Memories and a half! —Velhos tempos da Babilonia —Memories of Lanzarote, Canary Islands 1992, dancing in the Disco! —que recuerdo! gracias —unvergessliche zeiten! —Mis mejores años…gracias por el recuerdo. —this song is one good memory-lane stuff —Kindheitserin-nerungen werden geweckt :) —Hiermit beende ich meine kleine Musik-Nostalgie-Reise —The song takes me back to 42nd and 8th, late at night —che tempi quei tempi... —The first time I heard this song was on the way home from the mental ward I was put in after an overdose of vicodin, and grape kool-aid. The next day, I tried to hang myself. But the day after that, I heard this song for the second time, and it changed my life! —es eff yu arrrr Hans Overlander 1992 —reminds me of the southport dance weekenders back in the early 90s —My autobahn high speed song—... and a tripp down memory lane of happy nights dancing at Saxo nightclub in Paris...;) —The memories. 1999. Nightclub "the pub en ville" —Played this at a party in 99 while watching a gorgeous girl on a rock silhouetted against the rising sun dance like she was the only person there —So many wicked memories... Toronto Rave Scene & Warehouse Parties! Feels like a lifetime ago... Ohh To Be Young Again... —Ha ça rap-pel de sacre souvenir!!!! Remember Leeds 1998!!!! —I miss so much these times —I've been looking for this song for 10 years and one day, YouTube suggested it to me, thanks God you're too good. —Listened to this many times at the marble Mountain EM club Viet-nam 1969 —quel souvenir merci —I've searched for this record for so many years, since I've never know who is performing... singing just in my head for so many years —L'époque—raveing back in the day... —Noche de nostalgia :(—meu essa musica me lembra de quando eu era feliz e nao sabia haha —faz 10 anos ate encontrar —Moo nostalgia —Finalmente encontrei esta pérola!!!! tantos anos à procura!!!! :"""") —Italien 2009 Caneva..<33..immer der song..<3..yeah —oh epoca show de bola, sabiam criar musica... —ger nostalgitripp —Buenos recuerdos de epocas más simples —Just searched nostalgia on Google, and wow! I thought I was the only one that could smell and taste my memories from music. I thought there was something supernatural weird shit going on in my head, but damn it's called nostalgia!! You have no idea how long ive been trying to find out what my senses was! —Eu literalmente viajo com essa musica, tempos que nao voltam mais, overnight, toco, sunshine epoca de danceterias lotadas e boa musica, o oposto de hj onde essa porcaria de funk prevalece. Fica meu desabafo!! —Nostalgia level = over 9000 —Why nostalgia?? Can you explain a little bit, because I feel the same... —Oh my word this tune holds so many memories for me that will stay with me forever reminds me of the Empire Morcambe wat a place that was :) My first ever nite at the Empire I met this lad we bumped into each other nd that was that we made a real connection wat a nite that was one of my happiest :) Boy did he no how to party :) We stayed very much in touch after that 1st nite I have a lot of nice crazy memories :) Sadly he left this world 2 early I think of him always RIP M X —Tempo de verdadeiros djs o saudades —A trip down memory lane for sure... —Como tenho saudades daquele tempo —Que recuerdos!!! —wspomnienia... —Anni d'oro —Good old "b29" times :) —I'll never forget dancing to this song while sailing down the US Atlantic coast from New York to Florida as my brother steered and shook his head disapprovingly. —Keep making memories while listening to great music. It makes life that much better.

•

It's striking to observe, on this wall of recollections (these are also the millions of inner human murmurs heard by the angels in Wim

Wenders's *Wings of Desire*), that the same experience is described with almost equal frequency as both a source of sadness and a source of joy. Sometimes the richness of memory devalues a monotonous and threadbare present, sometimes it elevates the present by lending it an astonishing intensity. Melancholy's equivocal fullness is so difficult to express that we are always tempted to pin it down by relegating it to one of the two aspects inextricably entwined within it. Its most exact expression is the oxymoron, which holds closest to this ambiguity by preserving it: Gérard de Nerval's "black sun"; Victor Hugo's "pleasure of being sad."

•

In the internet there is a fountain of youth into which at first you drunkenly plunge your face, and then in the dawn light you see your reflection, battered by the years.

•

Proust established a clear distinction between voluntary and involuntary memory, a distinction which is partly demolished by our wanderings on the internet, the way they unfold in the recollection machine. On the internet, acts of voluntary memory often reach further than their initial goal, and it isn't unusual for them to confront us by chance, unexpectedly, with buried swaths of our past existence; epiphanies of involuntary memory draw the digital wanderer into new searches, where he seeks—voluntarily, now—to get his hands on another dose of the ecstatic recollection that so intensely transported him the first time.

[handwritten margin note: looking at pictures from the past can be nice in the moment reminiscing. But when you put the pictures away you are left with the feeling of how time has flown and how old you are.]

29

•

The recollection machine has strange effects. I don't know why each time I listen to excerpts from *Einstein on the Beach* on YouTube, and in particular "Knee Play No. 2," I remember an evening I spent with my father at the Comédie Française in November 1996—I had never heard Philip Glass and Bob Wilson's opera until I saw it staged in Paris in January 2014. Similarly, I ask myself why it is that whenever I listen to the instrumental version of "Last Dance in Copacabana" by Superfunk, I am beset by images of my first trip to Greece, in 2000—maybe I heard it in a bar at the time without paying it any attention, or maybe it was part of the distant sounds echoing from the island's only nightclub, now shut down. But I do know that I can retrieve voluntarily, with infallible efficacy, these involuntary associations that have the strength and charm of Proustian recollections.

•

Through the internet, we can see all things, read all things, hear all things. As for the sense of touch, "haptic technologies" are rapidly advancing; they can reproduce increasingly specific and diverse tactile sensations. Scents, for now, have eluded this duplication of all things in digital space. If in reading Hugo's lines "a fresh perfume suffused the tufts of asphodel," I become curious about these flowers, I can just as soon see on the closest available screen what these flowers look like and learn everything science has to say about them, but I can't smell their fragrance.

This is the rare impossibility that hasn't been overcome; scents are a remnant of the old world. We have no power to summon them; they are like those forgotten melodies which, in times past, would come back to mind only through little miracles that we might await for years. This "scent barrier" will certainly be broken as well. On that day, the last fortress of pure involuntary memory will have been conquered by the recollection machine.

We're working on it, at any rate; in all likelihood, we'll soon have machines similar to printers, equipped with a great number of little "odor cartridges," that will fill this gap in our total transformation of the world into reproducible memory.

3

PSYCHOPATHOLOGY OF DIGITAL LIFE, I.— F.: "More and more often, I feel as though I've lost touch with the objects of physical space. All around me, physical space is becoming a limbo, a huge attic in which objects randomly accumulate behind a closed door no one dares to open, terrified of the chaos that awaits on the other side. Before, I used to know in the blink of an eye where to find any one of my innumerable books; now it's much more difficult, just as my relation to all things I'm not connected to on the internet has become more difficult. On Google, I can't ask where I put my keys; I can't act upon them. I can't summon my books to my side. More and more actions are accomplished entirely on the internet; those that still require physical action have become strange and nearly impossible. If someone asks me to fill out forms and send them by mail, I become disoriented. It isn't familiar to me anymore. The thought of having to look for a paper I'm supposed to have in my possession causes me great anxiety. Everything that isn't digital suddenly seems fragile, lost, not to be grasped in any way, like trying to find a needle in a haystack. And when I have to sift through papers, either those that I've had for a long while or those that still arrive in too great a number, I tell myself with horror that all these insignificant documents that I'm about to throw away—cinema tickets, tourism brochures, old bank statements that I thought would one day compose a remarkably precise archive of my comings and goings, etc.—might in time have acquired considerable value, as they became traces, testimonies, spurs to recollection, and even, in a slightly more distant future, collectibles, historical documents, materials for a work of art. In digital *extension*—I can't help calling it that—at least we can keep everything without having to choose."

•

At the very moment I was putting the finishing touches on the above testimony, in a library in Paris's Latin Quarter, on April 11, 2014, a young woman came up to me and asked for a sheet of paper. As I was rummaging through my things while doubting out loud that I would be able to help, I finally extracted from the depths of my leather briefcase a pad of letter paper. She said, as if she'd already met with many refusals and fairly naturally expected I wouldn't be any better supplied than the other library visitors: "It's getting to be a rare commodity!"

•

Besides its ease and immediacy, writing an email rather than a paper letter has the advantage of being subject to no expense or tax, with the result that the simple act of sending a letter as in times past is beginning to enter the—little studied—category of formerly innocuous gestures that completely change in nature as they fall out of use and become exceptional signs of magnanimity, like spontaneously offering a cigarette to a stranger.

•

FOR THE RECORD. Fernand Braudel, in his vast book *The Mediterranean and the Mediterranean World in the Age of Philip II*, recalls that news of the St. Bartholomew's Day massacre, which had occurred on August 24, 1572, only reached Barcelona on September 3, and Madrid on the sixth. Long and unpredictable delays in the flow of mail were a constant obsession and immense burden for the kings and emperors of these past times; the entirety of political and economic life was a permanent struggle against the inherent slowness of space. Cardinal Rambouillet could write to Charles IX that the postmasters were so undiligent in delivering His Majesty's parcels that "by the time I receive them, both the season to profit from them myself and the occasion to execute their commands have often, to my very great regret, slipped by." The temporal significance of terrestrial space—as far as information is concerned—remains for us only on an infinitesimal level.

•

Google Maps can calculate fairly precisely how much time it takes to get from point A to point B, depending on whether you wish to walk, drive, bicycle, or take the train. Whenever I hit the wrong button and ask how much time it would take to *walk* from Paris to Marseille or La Rochelle, and the machine calculates the number of days required for such a trip, extravagant in our times, I feel as though I've suddenly been transported to the Middle Ages, or into Marguerite Yourcenar's *The Abyss*—and if my finger accidentally selects *bicycle*, silhouettes from 1940 appear in my mind's eye, as if our technical capacities had carried us to the top of a kind of watchtower, from which we could look back on the most distant past and see it rise at the edge of the landscape behind the last line of hills, like a troupe of minstrels, guildsmen, or penitents pursuing their long migrations through the forests and fields of Europe.

•

The Cartesian philosopher Nicolas Malebranche, in seeking to remain faithful to Descartes's thesis that mind and extension are mutually distinct, came to radical conclusions that had the appearance of impeccable rigor, but were so contrary to common sense that Descartes himself shrank from them: there is no communication whatsoever between mind and body; thought can only enter into relation with thought; therefore, we do not see bodies directly; we see them in God, through their ideas. These ideas of bodies are formed—or woven, as it were—in what Malebranche calls *intelligible extension*, the archetype of the material world we inhabit, and of an infinite number of other possible worlds.

It would go against the fundamental principles of Malebranche's philosophy to turn this *intelligible extension* into a conjunction, combination, or union of those two orders of being whose absolute separation, on the contrary, are fundamental to his innovation. But Malebranche's term possesses immense evocative power, enough to make us feel that we have, in a way, been led back to it by the emergence of this *digital extension* so ubiquitous and familiar we hardly notice how truly strange it is. And it would not be absurd to resort to ancient metaphysics to shed light on such strangeness—as if our new condition had spurred us to a grand retrospection, in which the most intricate and neglected speculations of the Scholastics regained the freshness of preliminary sketches, and suddenly resonated more with our own time than with the dark ages that gave birth to them.

•

As it happens, Malebranche—in another unexpected collision of epochs—often uses the term "consult" to refer to our relation to reason. For example, in his Elucidation Ten of *The Search After Truth*, we find the following sentence, which seems to prefigure our constant use of the Google search bar: "The Reason which man consults is infinite, since it cannot be exhausted, and it always has an answer to whatever is asked of it."

•

Bergson, in a few pages of *Creative Evolution*, gives free reign to an odd and remarkable thought experiment:

> Instead of acting, let us dream. At once the self is scattered; our past, which till then was gathered together in the indivisible impulsion it communicated to us, is broken up into a thousand recollections made external to one another. They give up interpenetrating as they become fixed. Our personality thus descends in the direction of space. [...] *Suppose for a moment that matter consists in this very movement pushed further and that physics is simply psychics inverted.* We shall now understand why the mind feels so at ease and moves

about so naturally in space, as soon as matter suggests the more distinct idea of it. This space is already possessed as an implicit idea in the mind's own eventual *detension*, that is to say, its own possible *extension*. The mind finds space in things, but could have got it without them if it had had imagination strong enough to push the inversion of its own natural movement to the end.

This reciprocal reversal of mind into matter, matter into mind, fairly aptly describes the slope of a daydream that becomes easier and easier to abandon oneself to, as our computer use invades every parcel of our existence. The screen world (the world to which the screen gives access) appears as a spatialization of the mind. The dream that the mind, as digital space, might gain control of physical space accompanies the experience of the internet like its shadow. That vague presentiment that sees the internet as a sign of the mind's growing mastery over physical space might explain (even more plausibly than the spirit of the times, which urges us to consider the Earth as the sole place where humanity might live and therefore limit our industrial productions so as not to ruin it) the surprising lack of general interest in the development of our capacities for interstellar travel. Previously, each revolution in our means of archiving and communicating—the printing press and the cinema—seemed to arrive with an equally remarkable conquest in the realm of material space: the discovery of America and the invention of aircraft.

•

COSMOLOGICAL MYTH (CIRCA AD 2500): "At the end of the Fifth Sun Age, the god Computer, weary of the forgetfulness and debauchery that reigned upon the Earth, swallowed all things and all living beings, and made them into eternal images that wandered through his entrails; but the goddess 3D Printer, taking pity upon these ghosts whose lamentations had reached her, lay with the god Computer, after which she gave birth once more to the inhabitants of the Earth, out of a new material in which the imperfections of the old bodies had vanished. Thus began the Sixth Sun Age."

•

Images have a destiny: to be projected beyond their creator's inner self onto a material medium, and then to be re-interiorized by the spectator. The more an image is reproduced, manipulated, unmoored, the more it enters the inner mind. When we digitize an old photograph and post it on the internet, we feel as though we are saving it, fulfilling its destiny, or at least winning an extra stage of destiny for it. The image now stands sheltered from random, irreversible destruction; it will be exhibited immediately to every gaze; it enters an ocean of text and images, giving rise to potentially infinite resonances.

More and more, however, this feeling is reversing course, as if we were entering a new dialectical phase. The flux of images has grown so rapid and vast that they vanish, engulfed in the wave almost as quickly as they appear. So we are seized by the desire to give them material form again, in order to hold them in our hands, as if the digital space that seemed to promise their salvation had once again left them fragile.

This reversal had already struck me several times, when one evening in October 2015 someone told me that a few months earlier he had created a start-up that offered to print out SMS conversations on little scrolls (and perhaps soon bind them into books as well, he added); his business was flourishing beyond all hopes.

•

PSYCHOPATHOLOGY OF DIGITAL LIFE, 2.—From F. again, a little later: "One day, I had to mail a letter. I was supposed to enclose a document. I had enough time to get to a postbox before the last pickup, which I couldn't miss if I wanted my letter to be accepted by the government office to which I was sending it. Everything was going well until the moment when, on my way to the postbox, I was seized by a doubt: Had I actually slipped the crucial document into the envelope? I looked at my sealed letter. It would have been complicated to reopen it—I would have had to start again with a new envelope, which would have taken quite a bit of time and made me miss the last pickup. I was faced with something absolutely impossible for me to verify, whereas if I had sent an email, I could have easily calmed my fears by checking the Sent folder.

"As I dropped the letter in the slot, I felt as though I were abandoning my destiny to a toss of the dice. I had forgotten how many blind spots there used to be in our connections to things, how many voids we had to step across, covering our eyes so as not to be paralyzed as we proceeded. This anguish concerning the contents of sealed letters that I'm about to mail took a particularly distinct form that day; but I had already experienced it in times past, and I have observed that it takes hold of me more and more often, as I write fewer and fewer paper letters."

•

PSYCHOPATHOLOGY OF DIGITAL LIFE, 3.—Still F.: "You already know that writing a paper letter has become an immense, disconcerting, insurmountable task for me. I fear my malady is reaching a new level. I get an idea for an email or a text message; I compose it in my head, sometimes down to the last detail; but the execution again seems crushing to me, painful, as if it were placing me at a distance from myself. Too often, I've resorted to Proust's lovely excuse in his letter to Madame de Caillavet, whose husband had fallen in battle: 'I've thought so much about that daughter of whom he was so proud, your dear Mademoiselle Simone, that I don't even know anymore if I actually wrote to her, so many times have I written her in thought.' The time has come for the inner, post-digital internet to deliver us from this gap between thought and act, mind and hand—one of the last vestigial features that still bind us to the tragedy of our original condition. The time has come for us to be able to write and send messages within our mind, without having to write them down on a physical device, with the help of our fingers."

•

Each of our five senses opens onto a realm as vast as the world; its limits are the limits of the world. The internet is the world, but it is not only the world (just as the world is not only images, smells, or sounds). The internet becoming an organ of sense is inscribed in its idea.

•

Tech experts are to the internet as chemists to nature.

•

[handwritten margin note: He goes out to focus be getting out does not distract him that way his phone can.]

Interiority is no longer master in its own house. The world has broken in and crowded it out. In the past, I only used to be able to concentrate at home, in silence and solitude. That's exactly what I have to get away from now if I want to have any hope of putting the hours of a day to good use; otherwise, I look up everything that crosses my mind on the internet; the brief distractions that normally punctuate a sustained effort take on outsize proportions; time slips through my fingers, and I watch myself waste the hours as I take long puffs of this opium. Physical space—definitely less teeming—is where I take refuge to regain my faculty for concentration. On a café terrace, the sound of motors, the merry-go-round of passersby, and even the neighboring conversations and the background music that used to irritate me, all these simple monotonous, regular, predictable things have become far more solid anchors for my attention than the solitude of an office or a room in which I know the infinite lies in reach of my laziness, musings, or lack of willpower.

•

The contemporary cult of the exhibition—a final, awkward act of resistance against each thing, and particularly art, having entered into the mind's inwardness—will have celebrated the dying embers of the reign of physical space, without either the priests or parishioners having been aware that they congregated in observance of the twilight of an era.

44

•

A final homage to physical space was rendered at the École Normale Supérieure in late 2013. But it was an open question, that evening, whether we had truly resolved to bid farewell to physical space, or whether we weren't rather expressing our unending attraction to it, one that we would never dare to cut off completely. I found myself there somewhat by chance. A digital exhibition devoted to Albert Camus had been installed in the library's oldest reading room. Vertical paper panels hung on the walls; each one had a 2D bar code that had to be photographed with a smartphone in order to access texts, images, or digitized sounds. But first, you had to download an app, and for a majority of the people who happened to be there, the thought of such a procedure only added to their original bafflement and discouraged them. Never since has an exhibition more purely accomplished its unavowed, essential function: to make us reunite with or meet our peers while enjoying a few sips of champagne. The exhibition wasn't only digital but also temporary; passing through the same room the next day I saw, to my great surprise, that everything had disappeared.

•

In the old days, old things, depending on how old they were, would be relegated to the past. Old photographs, old papers were dispatched to the back of an attic or the bottom of a drawer. The past's practical mode of existence in physical space was "at the bottom of." Such a phenomenon seemed to accord with a natural law. It was certainly possible to oppose this law by keeping before our eyes old things to which we were particularly attached, but in general a greater or lesser effort—physical and sometimes moral—was required in order to access images of the past.

Today, it's easy to find newspaper articles, forum discussions, photographs of our friends, and a number of other things that are several years old but do not in any way visibly differ from present things—neither by the speed at which we access them nor by the manner in which they appear. Through this compression of time, the past becomes a sort of parallel present; presents multiply like possible worlds.

•

What is the internet? A sign that the mind is not a lost dot in the universe, not a brief accident on the surface of hostile matter just waiting to blow it away like a speck of dust.

•

W., while reading a few of these notes, says: "Isn't this a kind of atheistic techno-spiritualism?"

I see no reason to object to such a characterization.

Spiritualism: I believe that matter is an aspect of mind; that mind is the future of matter; that matter will not hold out against its complete manipulation by mind. Or to put it otherwise: matter and mind are one and the same, but this unity realizes and reveals itself through time.

Techno-spiritualism: Mind is not ethereal; it does not move upon the waters. It exists only in those devices that trace at once the actuality of its limits and the potential of its unlimited expansion. The internet is not the mind, but it is "of" the mind. This spiritualism is not a humanism propped upon the current state of our biological being.

Atheistic: I hold religions to be transitory stages in the history of mind. They are noble monuments of the past, but they are destined in time to lose all purchase on knowledge and things. There exists a Christian techno-spiritualism, born with the revival of Teilhard de Chardin, which the emergence of the internet provoked in certain circles. I don't see God in the internet; I don't hope for the second coming of a cosmic Christ in the consummation of the noosphere.

●

What is the mind? The engine and medium of the metamorphosis of all things into memories, images, texts, aesthetic experiences.

●

We find it difficult to admit that phenomena whose existence depends upon boxes and electrical outlets could have any ontological value whatsoever. We want Being to stand on its own, to rest on nothing else. "And what if everything were shut off, then what would happen to this mind you're talking about?" And yet the intellect, as we have known it until now, has depended no less upon the life of human bodies, which, when broken, have immediately dragged it down into their own extinction.

47

4

IN THE LAST DAYS of October 2012, Hurricane Sandy ravaged the East Coast of the United States. Of all the catastrophes caused by the violence of wind and ocean, the shipwreck of the HMS *Bounty* particularly captured public attention. The HMS *Bounty* was a beautiful eighteenth-century frigate that had wandered into the twenty-first century. She was a replica, built in 1960 for the Hollywood film about the famous mutiny, starring Marlon Brando. The vessel still sailed and was often admired in parades of tall ships.

Late in the afternoon of October 25, she left the port of New London, Connecticut, in defiance of weather forecasts of the approaching hurricane; she was to sail to St. Petersburg, Florida, a crossing that would take several days.

For a little less than forty-eight hours, the *Bounty* advanced without too much hindrance. On October 27, she encountered very heavy seas, which continued to worsen. On the twenty-eighth, she faced thirty-foot waves and hundred-mile-per-hour winds. The vessel, whose structure was aging, took on water; but she was equipped with powerful bilge pumps that allowed her to make more or less normal headway. Nevertheless, there came a critical moment when the breaking waves deposited such a quantity of water that the bilge pumps couldn't evacuate it quickly enough to keep the engines and electric generators from being submerged—that is, the very equipment upon which the action of the pumps had depended. From then on, the *Bounty* was condemned to a slow sinking.

The Coast Guard was alerted to the situation by radio. On October 29, at around four or five o'clock in the morning, the crew donned survival suits and lowered the lifeboats. As they were counting off in the pitch-black night, they realized that, of the sixteen people who had been on board, two were missing: a female crew member around forty years old and the captain of the ship.

The Coast Guard didn't take long to spot the lifeboats. The survivors were hoisted into helicopters and brought to land. Search missions continued throughout the day to find the two missing crew members. The body of the woman was sighted during the afternoon, in open ocean; she had not survived. At around seven o'clock in the evening, in the last gleams of daylight, a helicopter flew over the *Bounty*, still half afloat; it wouldn't be long now before she sank. A single crew member remained missing: Captain Robin Walbridge.

A consideration of the circumstances surrounding this drama makes it seem like a story by Melville or Conrad. At sixty-three years of age, Captain Walbridge gave no impression of being a hothead—but we often forget that those men whose lives are behind them are sometimes the ones most capable of making decisions that would expose them to the risk of death. He had captained the *Bounty* for seventeen years. Everyone could testify to the extreme attachment he had to this strange ship, whose beauty, of course, had something kitsch about it in the eyes of real sailors, though it still drew their eyes, along with those of the public at large.

The investigation conducted after the shipwreck revealed that the shipyard where the *Bounty* had recently been dry-docked for routine maintenance had found significant hidden weaknesses that she had carried for many years. The captain was, apparently, shaken by this revelation. Even if she had remained in port, the *Bounty* could have been very seriously damaged by the hurricane. People imagined that his love for his ship had brought him to this mad gamble: to get away from the coast in time to reach a patch of open seas where the winds would be a little less strong. When the inquiry came to an end, American newspapers reported: *His desperation to save the ship ironically led to its destruction.*

Other facts, however, complicated this hypothesis. The *Bounty* had been up for sale for some time. She was having difficulty finding a buyer, even when her structural defects had not yet been detected. But had the transaction eventually taken place, there was no guarantee that the new owner would have kept Robin Walbridge as captain; perhaps the buyer might even have put an end to the *Bounty*'s journeys, converting her into a restaurant or theater, a floating pontoon permanently berthed at some pretty Maryland port where parents bring their children on Sundays. According to the survivors' testimony, the captain behaved in a strangely excited manner before and during the fatal crossing, in contrast to his usual prudence and calm. Even more troubling, in the midst of the navigation, he changed course ninety degrees, so that the *Bounty* crossed the path of the fiercest winds at a moment when she could still hope to make her way to a place where the storm, however fierce, was hardly the raging storm she would finally encounter.

The HMS *Bounty* had a Facebook page, which posted the progress of the rescue operations more rapidly than the traditional news sites. It expressed hopes; it broke bad news. The two series stood side by side on the wall's message history. When you scrolled down, you retrieved the joyful, tranquil atmosphere of the days and weeks that preceded the final voyage; many a photo of the *Bounty* was to be found here, taken in the end-of-summer sunlight along the East Coast of the United States. Everything was there, unchanged, like signs of the good life in Pompeii, turned to mockery beneath the ashes that preserved them intact for centuries. On the date of October 25, you could read this post: *Happy Birthday to Captain Robin Walbridge*...With Special Hugs & Kisses from his Family, S——, J—— and T——.

As I read this, tears came to my eyes. I was seized by an emotion that I felt was unprecedented, because it was the product of an arrangement of information that only the internet had made possible. At the same time, it reminded me of something. A little later, I managed to put my finger on a buried memory that had stirred within me but that I had been unable to identify. Toward the end of *Apocalypse Now*, as the patrol boat heading up the river approaches the lair of Colonel Kurtz, a young black crewman is killed by arrows fired by invisible attackers from behind a canopy of trees along the shore. He has been listening, on a pocket tape recorder, to a cassette of his mother's voice giving him news of home—we understand that she doesn't know how to write, or that he doesn't know how to read. As he lies at the bottom of the boat, the recording continues to roll, mechanically, and seems to envelop the boy's corpse in a spiritual shroud. I have always found this scene extremely moving. The tape recorder plays a powerful role; the reading of a handwritten letter would have been cut short in brutal but straightforward fashion; not so with this device, which allows communication to continue at the very moment when the two beings it is meant to link together have been irreversibly sundered. Suddenly, now, it is the ghost—the recorded voice—that is alive, crying alone in the wilderness, while the living man is dead. The loving and protective words uttered by the machine have not spared the child the violence of the world. We feel a profound injustice—an ontological injustice—in witnessing this powerlessness of love and its blindness to the tragedy that is taking place.

Only the film's narrative arrangement could place us in the presence of such a poignant coincidence. In real life, such a coincidence might not be absolutely improbable; but it would be very improbable for us to experience it, to see it. The situation is hyperbolic. It is a product of imagination, creation, screenwriting. Art has here assembled elements borrowed from reality and given them a finished form. In the story of the HMS *Bounty*, reality had already been set into a form, had already been narrated with unsettling perfection by this exhibited memory of the episodes, this cartography of time found in the spontaneous workings of the internet.

•

One day in 2013, while looking for news of a person I hadn't seen in years (he had a very beautiful sailboat from the 1930s, on which I had sailed), I came across his Facebook profile. The information was mostly public; we weren't "friends" on the site. In scrolling through the thread, I noticed there was a moment two years beforehand when the tone of the posts became different, enigmatic, more poetic. There were lyrics of a song by Georges Brassens ("Les Copains d'abord") and of another by David Bowie ("Space Oddity"). The transition was distinct, from wisecracks exchanged between friends to sudden melancholy thoughts laid upon the wall like flowers on a tomb. I suspected he had died during the few days

55

that separated the last schoolboyish message from the first moving one. Nothing, however, stated this explicitly; other hypotheses could fairly plausibly have been formulated: an illness, an accident, a tragedy that hadn't struck him but rather someone close to him, or else a radical change of existence, setting out on a solo circumnavigation of the world, exile in America or the South Seas. Recent messages had even been left by people who must not have been sensitive to the change of atmosphere on the page, probably friends even more distant than I, people who asked the dearly departed how he was doing, whether he might be interested in this or that, more than a year beyond the moment that to me seemed more and more clearly to be that of his death—of which I elsewhere found the sinister confirmation.

All at once, the image of the "thread" of life had become strangely concrete, along with the image of its breaking; and yet, beyond the instant at which this thread was broken, it continued as well; on the level of the page, there was a kind of equivalence between before and after, a relative lack of distinction between life and death that had confused other visitors. His digital existence continued to be lively. He no longer replied, but the mad hope that a message from him might appear on the wall had something bizarrely tangible about it. His absence was not so much that of someone deceased as that of a man plunged into a deep coma, half dead and half alive, around whom we gather in the hope that he will one day return to us—a situation that the advances of medicine have rendered more and more familiar in the past few years, at the same time as the internet was entering our lives.

•

In Romain Gary's *Promise at Dawn*, the hero receives countless letters from his mother urging him to be valiant and to heap glory
upon himself, as he fights in the forces of Free France. At the end of
the war, he realizes that she died three years before, and that these
letters were written and dated in advance, then entrusted to a friend
who mailed them at the proper times. I once dreamt up a scenario
about a blogger, who having foreseen or planned his own death,
programs the regular publication of his—previously composed—
blog posts for several years, during which time people continue to
believe he is alive. One could imagine any number of scenarios based
on the increasing possibility of multiplying the digital signs of a
life—whether one's own life after one's death, or the life of someone
else, in whose place one would publish these signs.

•

When my father died, I found myself in possession of his laptop
computer, on which his email account could be accessed without a
password. He was still receiving messages. This in-box inspired in
me a sort of holy terror that pushed me at once to glance furtively at
what was going on there and immediately close it again. Sometimes
the thought flashed through my mind of writing messages in his
place and, so to speak, prolonging his existence as an electrical phenomenon. In the eyes of a certain number of people whose relations
with him consisted essentially of email exchanges, he would have
continued to be what he was, exactly as before; his death wouldn't
have taken place. I could feel myself slipping into the belief that he
would in a sense survive; that the frontier between life and death
would be effaced or withdrawn. I knew this dream was empty, but

I was still haunted by its Faustian vision. I swung between tears and dread. This uncanny experience was possible only because the phenomenon that we become on the internet—our electronic phenomenon—confounds itself with our being in a far more radical way than all the traces and images we have left of ourselves for centuries.

•

It's becoming impossible to pass away. I don't mean pass away here as a synonym for death, but rather passing away in a literal sense of the phrase, as disappearing or going elsewhere, without implying the annihilation of the being who has gone. A being who has passed away hasn't ceased to exist; he is hidden or has disappeared. He has switched worlds. He has become a king in other latitudes. He's the uncle who set out for America; he's the French Foreign Legion soldier pardoned for his past. People speak of "disappearing without a trace," an expression that dramatizes its own meaning—hence its felicity—while also being slightly redundant: for anything that has left a trace, anything whose circumstances and causes of loss are known, cannot really be said to have "disappeared," to have entirely passed away. It's becoming more and more difficult to lose trace of anything whatsoever. The term *traceability*—born of the strict security standards imposed on the food industry—will soon apply to every domain of existence and become a general philosophical concept. Today we can be more or less certain that those who have passed away have not disappeared into another existence but are dead and gone. This increasingly inescapable certitude, however, doesn't deter the general public from sustaining the fantasy of some extraordinary feat, as if the ability to disappear were a kind of myth in which we still needed to believe. Xavier Dupont de Ligonnès and Malaysian Airlines Flight 370 incarnated this myth in the early 2010s.

•

The same naive desire to believe that someone could have the fortitude to remain out of sight of the internet—to remain untraceable—no doubt explains why, for a few months in 2014, a portion of the French public fell under the spell of a character who came out of nowhere and claimed to have made a fortune in the United States, even though no trace of him could be found either on social networks or in the alumni directories of the universities he claimed to have attended, or anywhere else. This paradox enveloped him in mystery and ended up making him even more seductive, since many people had begun to grow weary of the constant exhibition on social networks, and they were almost ready to see a role model in this exquisitely discreet multimillionaire. In reality, such an existential situation was impossible, ontologically impossible. In hindsight—says N., who closely followed this affair—it's peculiar that journalists continued to sing his praises and boast of the pharaonic projects his inexhaustible personal funds would finance, even after a list of the five hundred greatest fortunes in France had already been published on the internet, where he should have figured in due place, if he had been able to keep even a fraction of his promises.

•

"I believe," says Jacques Derrida in *Ghost Dance*, "that the future belongs to ghosts, and that modern technologies, of images,

59

cinematography, telecommunications, etc., augment the power of ghosts." In the same excerpt from this film in which Pascale Ogier asks him questions in his office at the École Normale Supérieure, Derrida declares: "I am the ghost." He slips into the image of himself that is being captured, even disappears behind it. It is this image that he lets speak in his place, or "ventrilocate" him, as he says.

In 2007 or 2008, a comment that accompanies this film on You-Tube—which I can't find anymore—noted that these claims have in a sense come into their own, making them all the more striking as we watch and listen to them now, when Derrida is dead even as these traces of him survive and continue to speak in digital space. The images speak true in designating themselves as ghosts—half-beings emanating from a past existence, deprived of the self-awareness of consciousness, perpetuating themselves in their own temporality, potentially eternal because no longer governed by the biological laws of life and death.

•

When he let himself be recorded at the beginning of the 1980s, Derrida was undoubtedly aware that his declaration would be truer—or, to put it otherwise, would hold a tighter and more robust link to its meaning—when he was no longer of this world. But he probably didn't have the slightest inkling of the future apparition and continuous development of this internet where his image permanently wanders, in a way that retrospectively makes his appeal to the notion of the ghost seem even more fitting. To utter a statement whose meaning is constantly reinforced by time, a statement whose truth was to be magnified in another era, a statement that calmly waited, motionless, without encountering the least resistance, for history to prove it right as surely as seedtime leads to harvest—that's a feat not just anyone can accomplish.

•

Those who think that the realization of the dream of immortality is now only a matter of time have speculated on the scenario of downloading—or backing up—the entire contents of our brain on an extremely powerful computer. But haven't we for centuries now been downloading the contents of our mind onto sheets of paper, by writing or drawing? Already in antiquity, the invention of literature coincided with the notion of the immortality of those who write—because people continue to read them and, in a certain sense, converse with them, long after their death.

•

People say that Kurzweil witnessed his father's death when he was around twenty years old, and that he stocked up all the traces he had of his father's life, in the hope of one day resurrecting an avatar with whom he could speak. But what is there of a person in his traces? What is there of a person in his traces, even if we reach a totality, a saturation, in the Great Downloading? As far as we know, we don't survive in our texts as spiritual animalcules, between or beneath the lines.

•

This argument can be inverted, by saying that the consigning of the contents of a mind to text is already the working model—even if it is so rudimentary—of a more perfect immortality that we should consider to be plausible, given the relative success of this first draft.

•

Since the late nineteenth century—since the simultaneous invention of aviation and cinema—we have witnessed an increasing convergence of humanity's dreams and its technical capabilities. We've become accustomed to crossing frontiers that didn't even seem approachable. Our dreams now find themselves, as it were, in the line of sight of our future ends.

•

The "marvelous" characterizes a world in which the gap between imagination and technique is at its widest. This is the world of medieval legends or of Eastern fables. The imagination defies the impossible by acting it out. The imagination is like a call for an unheard-of technology—a call which, a few centuries later, receives increasingly concrete and numerous responses. The story of Prince Ahmed, one of the tales of *The Thousand and One Nights*, has an ivory tube "furnished with a piece of glass at each end," in which one can see anything one wishes of all the things taking place everywhere in the universe. Another of these tales evokes an enchanted horse, half machine, half animal, with which one can fly very far if one knows how to turn a pin situated on its neck—a little like the ignition key on a motorcycle. Such representations, combining precise desires with the impossibility of achieving them, were unknown to Greco-Roman antiquity in its golden age. Imagination remained reasonable in the Greco-Roman world: it barely overflowed the bounds of nature or the feeble technical capacities of the time; it didn't invent that many incredible machines. The leap of imagination, which establishes the maximum gap between imagination and technique, also sets the reduction of this gap as the goal of the history of mind. We have now begun to live in the asymptotic stage of the curve that represents this gap.

5

IN *THE GHOST WRITER*, a Roman Polanski film I saw when it came out at the beginning of 2010, I was struck by a scene that appeared to be a slight flaw in the script—though I found the rest of the film very good. Two-thirds of the way through the film, in an oddly belated epiphany, the main character types into Google the name of a man he is suspicious of and sees his intuition confirmed by various facts that show up in the search results, things that would otherwise have remained unknown to him. You'd think he had just discovered the key to a safe, or the philosopher's stone, or some secret coffer anyway, containing rare, essential, classified information. The contents of the internet are, however, the least hidden and the most public thing in the world. But it's possible that this obvious fact was strangely overlooked for some time. I remember a period when, without anyone saying it aloud or even thinking it in a very direct way (I'm speaking here of those little furtive mental superstitions that lie beneath the threshold of direct consciousness), there was something almost shameful in resorting to the internet, at least in certain academic or scholarly circles, as if it was like taking a performance-enhancing drug for the mind, or looking up the answers at the back of your math book without having made the effort to solve the problem on your own. In the film, you could feel—unintentionally on the part of the screenwriter—the collision of two epochs: one in which people didn't have the reflex to consult the internet about everything, and one in which the first thing we do, more or less systematically, when we hear of something is to offer it up to the Google search bar.

•

Gone are the days when we used to feel a slight shame in saying we found something on the internet, as if it were an illicit or tainted source that an honest man couldn't mention without losing face—for an honest man already knows what needs to be known and always has: culture is, so to speak, a part of his being. I recently realized that it has become normal to specify in conversation, with a neutral voice, as if in passing, that we have learned from the internet the thing we are talking about, in order not to pretend to possess an extravagant amount of knowledge on our own. Soon, the internet will become so familiar that most of the time we won't even bother to mention it, no more than we say "I saw *in space* a flock of swallows"—or in general ascribe our perceptions to the sense organs that transmit them: we won't summon the internet out of its implicit obviousness to justify one piece of spontaneous knowledge or another.

•

It isn't yet so natural, however, to tell someone whom we have just met—or even someone we know well—that we have Googled him and therefore know a certain number of things about him, regardless of whether these things are flattering or embarrassing. This modesty causes awkward situations, which are becoming more and more noticeable and which will someday revolt against such modesty, relegating it to the category of obsolete scruples.

•

We tend to believe that our morals impose their laws on concrete situations. The emergence of the internet allows us to observe the contrary, almost as if we were witnessing a laboratory experiment: how an evolution of concrete situations forces our morals to redefine themselves, with such relentless necessity that we hardly notice it.

•

Social networks have already created the experience of a new moral landscape, in which self-exhibition has become the norm and therefore cannot be blamed in itself. This change of atmosphere is so universal that we aren't necessarily aware of it, or else we very quickly forget it. Judgment has not been abolished, but it rests on other nuances.

•

For some time after Facebook first began to spread, the act of *sending a friend request* retained a solemn significance, a relic of the importance we used to accord to this term in our prior forms of existence. We would often hesitate a long while before taking this step, for fear of making a tactless move or one that might be taken the wrong way. (No etiquette book had yet had time to include this in its explication of manners and lists of rules.) As for the person who received such a request, he had the sensation of exercising his power at the moment when he toyed with the idea of refusing, disdaining, or ignoring it. To have few friends could still pass for an exercise of aristocratic privilege. I remember one Saturday night on the Métro, late 2007 or early 2008, when some young people from Paris's sixteenth arrondissement, returning dead drunk from some party, addressed the entire subway car and announced that the following morning, magnanimous princes that they were, they would accept as Facebook friends all the nobodies who now had the honor of partaking in the epilogue to their noble drinking bout.

A few years later, returning to Facebook after a long absence, I realized that everything had changed. The important thing now was to have the greatest possible number of friends—even if you had never set eyes on them in your life. I didn't know when the transition had taken place. The internet had disclosed itself as a realm of measurement where everything received a number as the criterion of success. To send or accept a friend request had become something as innocuous as a handshake (but this also meant that refusing such a request was now almost as violent as refusing a hand-shake). A friend request was a fleeting instant in a perpetual flux. Number had conquered meaning; it had also simplified our lives.

•

It's boring to tend incrementally toward infinite friendships. We should start out by being friends with everyone, categorically. Only later would we perhaps proceed to a few cuts. We might be better people if our starting point of friendship was infinite.

•

At the beginning of René Daumal's *Mount Analogue*, the narrator, Theodore, receives a letter from a mysterious character, Pierre Sogol, whom he doesn't know and who asks to meet him. Theodore has written an article for a journal of esoteric studies, in which he evokes the myth—common to many cultures—of a gigantic secret mountain forbidden to mortals, because it is the lair of the divine. This mountain, he writes, must exist, and it must exist somewhere in the Southern Hemisphere to counterbalance the enormous mass of mountains in the Northern Hemisphere. There must, in other words, be something in the south that weighs as much as the Himalayas, the Alps, the Urals, etc., and it must rest on none of the known expanses of this earth—it must therefore be something condensed, in the form of a single mountain hidden from sight by some unknown phenomenon. The above reasoning is an attempt to deduce a natural fact abstractly— and, so to speak, mathematically, that is, by *analogy*. Theodore confesses that his text was only half serious and that he had already ceased to concern himself with it when Pierre Sogol wrote to him. Sogol, however, does not take this subject lightly; he has devoted his entire life to it. He has had occasion to carry his investigation much further: he has determined the location of the mountain; he has developed an optical theory to explain why no one has ever seen it; and he has begun to organize an expedition. He invites Theodore to join this small group that is about to set sail for the South Seas aboard the yacht of a billionaire friend. Theodore accepts; a few months later, the explorers disembark at the foot of Mount Analogue and begin their ascent (the death of Daumal interrupts the course of the novel at this point).

One day the internet confronted me with the outline of a similar plot. In 2006, I had published in the journal *Trafic* an article on *Purple Noon*, the film by René Clément, in which I teased out the thread of an interpretative reverie according to which the character Tom Ripley, played by Alain Delon, has something so enigmatic about him that it's tempting to wonder if he might have sprung from the depths of Atlantis. The article was entitled "The Atlantean Aboard the *Marge*." It wasn't difficult to find traces of it on the internet and to contact me; that's how, at the end of 2012, I received an email from a certain F.D., whom I didn't know. The subject line read: "Who's the barbarian?" The message was as follows:

Mr. Maël Renouard:

The enigma of Atlantis has been solved for over ten years now. Why then are you still unaware of this?

Sincerely,
F.D.

A brief internet search informed me that my correspondent had written a book, probably self-published, in which he claimed that the great myths of humanity were the expression of a fetal memory of intrauterine life. According to this doctrine, the serpent represented the umbilical cord; the tree of life, the placenta; the deluge, the prenatal breaking of the amniotic fluid; and so on. As for Atlantis, we should see it as a kind of variant of the Garden of Eden which, according to the author, was itself nothing more than an image of the fetal world that had vanished at birth. In support of this hypothesis, the Pillars of Hercules, beyond which the Greeks located the sunken continent, represented the entrance to the uterus.

Indeed, I was unfamiliar with this thinker and his work; I inferred from this that the barbarian was me. Saddest of all, such a theory obviously ruled out any geographical identification of Atlantis and any attempt to explore its last vestiges: there would be no expedition to the Azores on a majestic schooner.

A little later, still piqued by the curiosity this episode had awakened, I read a blog post harshly critiquing F.D.'s "inept" interpretations: "a sea of sheer delusion [...] Nostradamus *cum* psychoanalyst." The critique seemed to issue from a rational mind; the style was poised and articulate, with occasional polemical outbursts; but as I read on, I realized that what this naysayer principally had against F.D. was his claim to have disproved the existence of Atlantis as an actual earthly place, long confirmed by the most reputable studies. The craziest person isn't always who you think, and there's still a chance that some shadowy characters will roam the seas in search of Atlantis and invite me to join their crew.

•

The invention of a fictional plot—novel or film—that unfolds realistically in the contemporary world can no longer neglect to represent the internet's total intrusion into the slightest acts of our existence. This results in an unprecedented tension with works of the past, which, along with one's own life, are the other natural source of inspiration for the creator of a story. Like every craft, this work passed down recipes and models. Until recently, the two sources— tradition and observation—could be exploited harmoniously, or at

73

least without conflict. Today, when the story maker refers to past models—whether twenty or five hundred years old—he feels a strange separation, the lack of a firm hold, as if a sheet of glass lay between him and these representations of a pre-digital world. This is certainly not the first time that new objects have changed our way of life and that writers have asked themselves what they should make of them. But the nature of the present modification is different.

At the beginning of the twentieth century, people debated whether the plane, the automobile, the telephone were noble enough to appear in literature. These empty quarrels were swept away by obvious successes. To pose such a question today in regard to the internet would be even more ridiculous: not only has experience shown us that the disdainful exclusion of modern technical phenomena from artistic depiction is rarely the hallmark of an outstanding work but also, and especially, the current transformation concerns something that is fundamentally far too vast to be designated simply as a "new object" added to the world, which we might choose to use or not. A character has never been obliged to board a plane, even after air travel became widely accessible. The automobile and the telephone, though more pervasive, haven't affected each moment and each aspect of our existence as the internet has. I have no difficulty imagining a three-hundred-page novel written and set in 1990, in which not a single telephone would be heard to ring. I don't even think this would have constituted a feat or a stylistic exercise. But the internet has become so coextensive with all our mental acts, with all our moments—of boredom, idleness, frantic work, philosophical reflection, personal anxiety—that a character in the 2010s who was deprived of its use for one reason or another couldn't fail to be obsessed by its absence. This radical newness, which introduces a noticeable discontinuity in the long tradition of the craft of storytelling, also opens the way for the invention of unheard-of plots, the abundance of which we do not yet fully grasp.

•

A surprising number of today's novels—whether fiction or auto-fiction—are not set in the present moment, or in an unspecified time that might as well be the present, but rather in the recent past, the 1980s or 1990s, when daily life largely resembled the world we know today, except that the internet was absent, as if there were a threshold here that we refused to cross, a dangerous territory for writing, for style, something that we shied away from facing, or that we were afraid we might not be able do, an abyss toward which we could feel ourselves proceeding, before slamming on the brakes at the last second and stopping on the brink. It seems to me that this phenomenon, which is probably unconscious most of the time, comes just as often from writers who are relatively old—or at least have lived the greater part of their existence before the internet—as from novelists who are young but perhaps too literary to resign themselves to creating plots in which the invasive irruption of this element would make them feel they were devastatingly cut off from their past models. Paradoxically, the internet fosters precisely such a tendency toward historical novels set in the recent past when it didn't exist, because it constitutes a marvelously accessible and nearly inexhaustible—or at least richer and richer—source of information about the periods before it came to be.

•

It has often been said that Aurélien Bellanger's *Théorie de l'infor-mation*, released in the autumn of 2012, was the first novel of the internet age in France. This is indeed its explicit theme. But one can't help thinking that a first encounter between the internet and literature took place a few years earlier, in a subterranean way, with-out anyone noticing, when the French version of *Schott's Original Miscellany* was published in 2005 and Jonathan Littell's *The Kindly Ones* came out in 2006. It's not impossible that these authors learned how to use the internet earlier than their readers, and that for a time an asymmetry arose—unprecedented in the history of literature, and equalized since—between the means the author has at his dis-position and those the reader attributes to him. It's also not impos-sible that they hardly resorted to the internet at all. However that may be, these are the last books in which we admired feats of eru-dition that are now within reach of almost anyone. They inaugu-rated an era in which their singularity became universal, an era that would soon cast an indifferent eye on the immense hoard of infor-mation for which they were celebrated.

•

Precision has become too easy; the anguish of the blank page has been almost completely eradicated from our lands. The work of writing has suddenly come to resemble that of sculpture, whose entire material is given at the outset and whose motto is: Chisel away. The accumulation of details found on the internet backfires against the realist ambition that naively motivates it, because these details ring false. We have to cast aside entire cargos of useless spe-cifics. We have to strive to be vague.

•

When he was working on *Sentimental Education* at the end of the
1860s, Flaubert asked his friend Jules Duplan to assemble an
extremely detailed report on the modes of transportation and communication that existed at the time of the 1848 revolution; he
needed stagecoach schedules, company names, routes; he particularly wanted to know how one could return from Fontainebleau to
Paris at the moment when the riots were raging. It's said that this
whole mountain of information gave birth to a single little sentence:
"Leloir's mail-coach had just left, Lecomte's berlins were not running, while the stagecoach from the Bourbonnais would not be
passing until late at night and might be full."

I didn't know this anecdote when, in a short story, I invented the
character of a young diplomat on assignment in Alexandria who
returns to Paris in June 1871, toward the end of a catastrophic year
for France: the country has been defeated; the Empire overthrown;
the Commune crushed. The internet, playing the role of Jules
Duplan, informed me that the crossing would realistically have to
take place aboard a steamer of the Messageries Maritimes, which
until the very recent fall of Napoleon III had been called the Messageries Impériales. I couldn't resist noting this name change in the
story; later, I deleted that detail while proofreading the text for the
*n*th time, as I realized the whole story was bogged down by a thousand such historical facts I had accumulated with naive joy, thanks
in large part to the internet, without having managed to restrain the
arm of the omniscient narrator in time.

•

In rereading *Missing Person* a few days after Patrick Modiano won the Nobel Prize at the beginning of October 2014, a question crossed my mind toward the middle of the book and haunted my reading till the end: How could we possibly have accepted, for so many centuries, that we were forgetting so many melodies and the names of so many faces?

•

F.: "A writer like Modiano has become impossible, now that we know everything about everyone and nothing is threatened with absolute oblivion."

H.: "One day, email will be a hundred years old. Then two hundred, three hundred, etc. Philosophy or literature scholars in the year 2500 will unearth forgotten or deleted emails the authors they are working on wrote several centuries earlier. Facebook, too, will be a hundred years old, even if everyone abandons it long before then. As a thing of the past, it will continue to wander the internet, and its aesthetic charm, more or less nonexistent today, will have increased tenfold through its falling into disuse. People will say: I found an old Facebook profile from fifty years ago, from two hundred years ago. We find this hard to imagine, and yet it will come to pass. A writer like Modiano, therefore, hasn't become impossible. A Modiano of the year 2080 will create plots and atmospheres out of peculiar friend connections, "blanks" in a biography time line, or a few photographs that have been online for decades and in which one often sees—particularly at some grand parties that took place on avenue Marceau in 2025—a single pensive face whose name, mysteriously, has never been *tagged*.

•

Chateaubriand had his grave established on a little island exposed to the sea, facing Saint-Malo. His name isn't written anywhere. A plaque nevertheless states that a "great French writer" lies here, and enjoins visitors to respect the austere quietude that he selected for himself for all eternity. Apparently, this plaque was laid long after Chateaubriand's burial, but it vividly corresponds to his turn of mind, a combination of naive fatuousness and obsessive consciousness of the void. This chronicler of past grandeurs, this solitary voyager touched with emotion at the sight of stelae with now-illegible names, never ceased to cry that human memory would obliterate him from its records—but he did so in the manner of those brilliant students who, to ward off failure and attract success as a reward for their humility, lament time and again that they have botched their homework and still receive time and again the highest grade, to their classmates' great chagrin. He certainly didn't imagine that one day there would be people who wouldn't know whose grave was marked by this anonymous stone.

I've been there a few times, on that Grand Bé which you can reach on foot at ebb tide; one summer afternoon, lying on the grass a few yards from the stela, I watched the promenaders disconcerted by this unexpected Trivial Pursuit question. This was before the invention of smartphones. They sifted through their old schoolboy memories trying to save face in front of their children. "A great French writer...Let me see...Victor Hugo?...Balzac?...Molière?..."

Chateaubriand's vainglorious modesty has been punished enough; technology has put an end to his purgatory. His ghost's oft-burning ears must have been somewhat soothed by the apparition of this new race of passersby that has the capacity to know everything about anything it lays eyes upon.

●

Félicité, the servant with a "simple heart" in Flaubert's story of the same name, has a nephew whom she loves like a son: Victor, a sailor. She learns one day that he has put in at Havana. This name evokes a few images of Épinal, but she has no notion of geography. To learn a little more about it, she goes to consult M. Bourais, who is educated. This happens at the beginning of the 1820s in Pont-l'Évêque. Bourais opens an atlas and shows her a little black dot.

> Félicité peered closely at the map; the network of colored lines was a strain on her eyes, but it told her nothing. Bourais asked her what was puzzling her and she asked him if he would show her the house in which Victor was living. Bourais raised his arms in the air, sneezed and roared with laughter, delighted to come across someone so simple-minded. Félicité, whose understanding was so limited that she probably even expected to see a picture of her nephew, could not understand what was so funny.

Google Earth and Facebook have rung in the revenge of simple hearts who believe in real presence. The internet has vindicated the faith of the ignorant who imagine that knowledge is integral—that to know, is to know everything.

●

The Duke of Nemours saw a great light in the bower. All the windows of it were open; slipping along by the side of the palisade, he came up close to it, and one may easily judge what were the emotions of his heart at that instant: he took his station behind one of the windows, which served him conveniently to see what the Princess of Clèves was doing. He saw she was alone; he saw her so inimitably beautiful, that he could scarce govern the transports which that sight gave him. The weather was hot, her head and neck were uncovered, and her hair hung carelessly about her. She lay on a couch with a table before her, on which she had set her computer; the Duke of Nemours, observing the figures that formed themselves upon the screen, perceived that she was writing an email. He was at too great a distance, however, to see who was to receive it, or of what matter it treated. Whether she allowed her mind to wander, or that she expressed her thoughts with difficulty, long moments passed between each stroke of her fingers upon the keyboard. She seemed at last to have finished her work, or at the very least to have interrupted it; for he saw her transport herself to a new window upon the screen. She must have entered the Duke of Nemours's name in the Google search bar, for several images of the Duke appeared; she clicked on one of them, which became truly large, and she looked upon it with an attention and thoughtfulness which only love can give. It is impossible to express what the Duke of Nemours felt at this moment; to see, at midnight, in the finest place in the world, a lady he adored, to see her without her knowing that he saw her, and to find her wholly taken up with things related to him, and to the passion which she concealed from him; this is what was never tasted nor imagined by any other lover.

6

IN EARLY 2010, when I was working for the prime minister at Matignon, I was asked to prepare the draft of a speech extending "New Year's wishes to the general secretariat of the government." I hadn't been there for long; I didn't really know what form this exercise should take; the instructions I had been given were vague, and I knew it would be useless to try to obtain anything clearer. I would have liked to see one or two examples of previous speeches. On the off chance that some archives might be lingering there, I did a Google search. Sure enough, I found a great many things, more than I had imagined; I was even surprised to discover that this event, unknown to the public at large and more or less pointless, had been so well documented. I glanced at two or three speeches offered by links on the first results page. It was official prose, of a kind I had already seen heaps of since my arrival at Matignon. A few turns of phrase, however, seemed unusual. From time to time, there were metaphors that didn't belong to the stock of commonplaces I had learned my way around. And yet these too had a stereotypical look, as if signaling that they belonged to a distinct world, possessed of its own stock of commonplaces. There was nothing striking enough to give definite form to my uneasiness; the incongruity remained imperceptible.

I began to have more serious doubts about the nature of the texts

I was reading when, in a repeated and completely natural way, I saw the term *primature* start to appear. Such a term, to my knowledge, has never been used in France to designate the prime minister's residence or the political entity that envelopes—but is not equivalent to—the physical person who holds this position. I even admit that it took me a little while to understand what the term meant—that *primature* must be a synonym of sorts for *Matignon*. Perhaps the relatively rare or esoteric use of this word had escaped me all these years, despite a fairly studious childhood during which I had begun reading *Le Monde* in lycée and had later worn out my eyes on many a history book. And I was ready to lament, as the old recrimination against the elite goes, that it's really true "they" don't tell us everything, "they" hide things from us, things I would never have known if life's twists and turns hadn't brought me across the threshold of these decidedly mysterious circles. Unless it might be more fitting—I considered this as well—to blame my endless capacity for forgetfulness and distraction.

Or perhaps the expression had been introduced only recently, without my noticing it, and without anyone having seen fit to inform me of it, since it was obvious. It was fairly common, after all, for new words to appear; for example, *gouvernance* had entered everyday vocabulary in the mid-2000s. It was said that Jean-Pierre Raffarin, the prime minister at the time, had done much toward the term's adoption. Perhaps he had also worked to have people adopt the term *primature*, at least in certain administrative circles? Did the term *primature* stand to *Matignon* in the same relation as *gouvernance* to *gouvernement*: a semantic novelty, a chic modern variation? It was nothing new, in the world of politics, for people to believe they were having an effect upon things by priding themselves on modifying the vocabulary; and it was far from rare for such attempts to meet with no success among public opinion or the media.

I was aware of the far-fetched nature of all these surmises, and I took amusement in them as they filed past. Then I looked more closely at the addresses of the links that Google had offered me and that I hadn't yet finished consulting. I hadn't paid close enough attention to the fact that they didn't end in ".fr" but rather in ".bj," ".ci," ".bf," ".sn," ".ma," or ".ml." And so the texts I had before me or that I was about to read came from various African countries—Benin, Ivory Coast, Burkina Faso, Senegal, Morocco, Mali—whose institutions, established after independence, had been largely inspired by those of France. And along with the institutions, they had replicated the ceremonies, the mutual cordialities between "constituted bodies," the formulas of address—deferential and as long as your arm—at the beginning of speeches, an entire series of obligatory passages proper to the rhetoric of power.

This phenomenon provoked in me a strange aesthetic emotion, which, in the final analysis, was less historical or political than metaphysical. It wasn't a question of Europe, Africa, or the twentieth century. It was a feeling of multiple worlds. Worlds spun in circles before my eyes on the Google results page. They lived parallel lives at gigantic distances. It was a feeling of infinity. I abandoned myself to wistful mathematics: if there were at least a dozen worlds in which one could confirm the existence of a "general secretariat of the government," then the presence of life and even intelligence on other planets became highly probable.

I thought of Leibniz's phrase—"It seems that in Harlequin's empire of the moon, everything is just like here"—and at the same time, I remembered something else, a memory that escaped my grasp, an analogy that at first I couldn't identify, but which fairly quickly surfaced in my memory. When I was a child, I had been very taken with an episode of *Star Trek*—the only episode, in fact, of which I retain a relatively clear memory today—in which the crew of the mothership disembarks on a planet whose inhabitants, while possessing advanced technology, automobiles, etc., live as in Roman antiquity, wearing togas and practicing cruel circus games that have to be brought into line, for I believe that this was the mission of the heroes on that particular day. Such an association of ideas might not be as absurd as it seems, for there was something Leibnizian about *Star Trek*, in its infinitely inhabited infinite space, its ideal of interplanetary federalism, and the universal rationality that ruled all these worlds, the combination of familiarity and difference that was to be found all the way to the edges of the universe. And so I imagined distant planets sown throughout an infinite number of galaxies and each possessing its own "general secretariat of the government": over there, under other stars, amid palaces with unfathomable forms, humanoids in space suits would exchange New Year's greetings while speaking like senior officials of the French Fifth Republic, each time they completed a full rounding of their sun.

And for a few days, I had a whim to introduce the word *primature* in France by playfully smuggling it into certain speeches; I did nothing of the sort.

•

Wikipedia multiplies the number of worlds by placing them on equal footing. Present worlds, past worlds, imaginary worlds, virtual worlds that never came into being—all are treated in the same way and presented in identical form. The French administrative departments of Holland and Italy under the reign of Napoleon have their entries, with their capital cities, their successive rulers, their maps, etc., exactly like those in which we live. The ephemeral world of a France with a hundred and thirty administrative departments—that past potentiality which was not to be—has, *sub specie vicipædiae*, the same apparent consistency as the fifty states of the United States. Many ghostly worlds thus regain a spiritual tangibility and hover around the present.

•

This encyclopedia into which everything can enter, regardless of its mode of existence, and be exhibited according to the same protocol, is probably the strongest illustration of Tristan Garcia's "flat ontology" according to which all things, insofar as they are equally things, are considered without hierarchy of metaphysical origin—in other words, democratically.

•

We can live in many worlds, in many languages. There is an internet Pentecost that makes us speak in tongues and will soon cast aside, among other terrors of the past, the dystopia of a world dominated by Anglophone monolingualism.

•

We used to feel that language use consisted in associating elementary units in order to compose statements or express a meaning. Meaning had to be created ex nihilo. The internet has altered this image of language by offering an immense stock of already formed statements in every language—by presenting itself, in a way, as an infinite phrase book. Everything has been said, and we only have to draw from the depths of this reservoir the already deposited phrase—from five, twenty, or three hundred years ago—that corresponds as adequately as possible to the context in which we want to speak.

•

A new art language is being created, a language whose elementary units are complex sequences drawn from previous works, a little like the process of integration in mathematics, or as if organisms were to become atoms in higher-level organisms: sampling in music is, to a certain extent, the emblem of this phenomenon.

•

John Searle, at the beginning of the 1980s, formulated a thought experiment known as the Chinese room argument, which was meant to counter what he saw as a naively enthusiastic conception of artificial intelligence.

Suppose, he said, that we are locked in a room and given a basket of Chinese characters—a language of which we are entirely ignorant—and provided with a manual explaining how to arrange them so as to compose correct statements. Now suppose that people outside the room slip us new sets of characters beneath the door (which they call "questions," but which we can't even recognize as such). Thanks to our manual, we are able to associate these with characters that we draw from our basket and then send to our unknown interlocutors, who perceive them as "answers." We behave, in their eyes, as if we understood Chinese, whereas we don't know a single word of it.

According to Searle, computers are in a similar situation; when they react to a signal, they have has no consciousness of its meaning, no intentionality. From this point of view, it is false to ascribe artificial intelligence to a machine, just as it is false to yield to the opposite temptation and liken the functioning of our mind to that of a computer. Even if it were to pass the famous Turing test—of which the Chinese room is a parody—a computer affords only a semblance of understanding, with nothing behind it, absolutely nothing that truly relates to what, for us, is thinking.

At the beginning of 2014, I had the idea to enrich the Chinese Wikipedia entry of a historical figure whose biography I knew, simply by linking him to categories such as "alumnus of such and such university" and "twentieth-century French writer (or physicist, or mathematician)" and "Nobel laureate in such and such discipline," etc. I don't know a single word of Chinese. But by toggling between various French and Chinese web pages, I fairly quickly managed to mark out the units of symbols that corresponded to the expressions I was looking for; then I copied and pasted them in the proper locations. I was, and still am, incapable of pronouncing the characters I handled in this way. As in the parable of the Chinese room, someone who had seen me working, from another computer screen on the other side of the world, or else passing behind me and peering over my shoulder, would probably have thought that I knew Chinese; now, I didn't know Chinese at all, but I knew perfectly well what I was trying to express with a few of its characters.

7

"The finest catastrophe, better even than the sinking of the *Titanic*, occurred in the night of 31 December 1899, the first night of the century. The liner fitted out by the city of Manaos, then rich on its profits from the rubber industry, had sailed way up the Amazon river, with the whole world's gentry and stars on board, for the most luxurious of international parties. These members of high society drank and danced all night to the rhythm of the bands, as the liner slowly drifted off and became lost in the labyrinth of the forest. They ran aground in one of the innumerable tentacles of the river and were not found until much later, by which time they had all died of hunger, thirst and the heat. In this way, a part of the world's elite was offered up as a human sacrifice to the new century. *Manus deus*—Manaos—malefic consonance.

"Not only did they disappear, but even this story has disappeared from the archives. I've never been able to track it down myself. Did I hallucinate it out of boredom, or as an effect of the heat? No, I'm sure I read it as a genuine item of information. Why isn't it in everyone's memory, like the story of the *Titanic*?"

Jean Baudrillard wrote this in *Cool Memories II, 1987–1990*. This catastrophe seems to have haunted him; he returned to it in the next volume of the series, *Fragments: Cool Memories III, 1990–1995*, but more briefly, without having managed to uncover any additional information. It is not impossible that it appears elsewhere in his work.

If Baudrillard had had access to the internet at the time, he would have typed into the Google search bar "Manaos steamship river 31 December 1899 deaths," or something of the sort. He would have immediately known what he had in hand—hallucination or positive fact. Today it's very simple, incredibly simple, to answer this question that a person from the pre-digital age would undoubtedly have taken months to pursue seriously, "exhausting the bookshelves" of several South American libraries, as Borges would say.

When you do such an internet search today, you only come upon the very Baudrillard texts I have just quoted; no other source reports such an event. Nor do you find anything that remotely resembles it; not a single vaguely related story that might have sown the seed of the fantasy. One wonders if Baudrillard was playing a trick on his readers, or if he hoped to instigate endless daydreams and inquiries—a little like Voltaire, when he told the story of the iron mask in *The Age of Louis XIV*.

But it used to be easier to plant fantastical events in the collective memory; the passage of time was all it took for people to find a rational explanation to scanty evidence or simple forgetfulness. Origins were quickly lost in the mist. A book could be the sole custodian of a secret, or pretend to be so. Now, everything that crops up can be subjected to cross-checks that leave little room for dreams to crystallize, little room for that gradual process by which one sees a story like that of the iron mask acquire, over time, an amplitude, a consistency, a quasi-reality that arises simply from the speculations or inquiries that multiply around it. In a world without internet, a reader in the year 2050 who happened upon this page of *Cool Mem-*

ories would have had many more reasons to believe in this catastrophe than to not believe—he would probably even have had every reason to want to believe it.

One day, *Fitzcarraldo*, Werner Herzog's film released in 1982, came up in conversation with a friend. It tells the story of an adventurer who has the mad plan to build an opera house in the heart of the Peruvian rain forest, in the city of Iquitos. His model is the Teatro Amazonas, built—as it happens—in Manaus during the 1890s thanks to money from the rubber trade; at the beginning of the film, Fitzcarraldo attends a dazzling performance of an opera by Verdi there. To raise funds, he buys himself a concession of rubber-tree land, the only one still on offer as it is known to be almost inaccessible. He hopes to force a passage by hauling a ship over land for several hundred yards, between two branches of the Amazon, with the help of natives who live in the jungle. He buys an old steamship, reequips it, and embarks. The expedition, despite epic twists and turns, is a failure. In the end, he stages an opera performance—one time only and dreamlike—aboard his boat as it drifts down the river.

I had seen this film long ago, too long for its memory to surface opportunely while reading Baudrillard's text. Baudrillard's story of a ship lost in the meanders of the Amazon had vaguely reminded me of something, something I had been unable to identify until the coincidence of this conversation called to mind the plot of *Fitzcarraldo*. Obviously, this was the source of Baudrillard's phantasmagoria. He must have unknowingly transfigured the vision of this film into the dream of a real event.

There might be still further influences. The presence of high society on a luxury steamship evokes the inauguration of the Suez

Canal at the end of 1869 and of the Panama Canal in the summer of 1914, both of which were cause for prodigious celebrations and considerable sumptuary expenses. The global elite, invited in large numbers, weren't sacrificed there; but one can't help remembering that these gigantic festivities were very soon followed by devastations and geopolitical upheavals that made a mockery of them and even relegated them to profound oblivion, as if "the hand of God" had afflicted humanity by condemning it to expiate its frivolity and industrious ambition through the horrors of war.

•

In *A Student's Guide to Intellectual Work*, Jean Guitton tells of one of his friends who took great pains to write a brief text but then published it in a little provincial review, precisely because the mere prospect of being delivered unto the gaze of unknown and potentially innumerable readers terrified him. "In this way he enjoyed the satisfaction of seeing himself published, without the fear of being read," writes Guitton, quoting him. In coming upon this happy phrase, one cannot help thinking of an entire category of university writings whose confidentiality has perhaps become so reassuring that their authors have ceased to worry about being read—even by their peers, who must likewise have ended up telling themselves they had better things to do. These authors seem to count themselves fairly lucky to add a line to their list of publications, while their articles or works join, without a single stranger's eye having fallen upon their pages, the obscure shelves of libraries where no one will come to disturb them for all eternity. One also cannot help thinking that the book—the book form, the codex, as opposed to the immediate exhibition characteristic of the internet—appears less and less as a means of making a text public and, strangely enough, more and more as an obstacle to reading, or, to put it otherwise, as a sanctuary, a distant and secret refuge protected from the curiosity of readers.

•

Many texts published in specialized journals that could only be found by rooting through the bookshelves of university libraries have regained a stunning presence by becoming immediately accessible online. This resurrection of texts exposes them to a kind of Last Judgment. There is a latent tribunal in digital exhibition. According to the Platonic myth, when the souls of the dead appear before the court of Minos, Aeacus, and Rhadamanthys, no corpse remains to conceal their secrets, their profound wickedness or unrecognized goodness; they are stripped naked, constrained to pitiless transparency. The same goes for these digitized texts that can no longer conceal themselves within a closed block of paper, behind opaque book covers, in the depths of labyrinthine libraries.

In November 2014, Michel Charles published a story on the *Fabula* website that would make for remarkable fiction (except it is true). He recounts how, as the director of a prestigious literary studies journal, he received an article—devoted to the "poetics of the anodyne"—from a certain R.-L. Etienne Barnett, an American academic with an apparently very ample résumé, who of course submitted the article in the hope that it would be published. Intrigued by certain stylistic oddities, Charles did an internet search and immediately discovered that a version of this text had already been published elsewhere, without the oddities, by someone else. He carried on with his inquiry and brought to light more than a dozen cases in which this author had either appropriated an article that was not his—by changing the title and introducing a few preciosities inspired by the worst kind of poststructuralism—or else republished, with a few variations here as well, a text of his own that had already been published (but it would be no surprise if these instances of self-plagiarism were themselves founded upon a provisionally untraceable initial act of plagiarism).

The man boasted of a great many publications; he claimed to belong to numerous boards, commissions, committees, societies, etc. Several things, however, were troubling. Such an obsessive listing of titles might have brought to mind the business cards of fortune-tellers—if it weren't a current practice among respectable figures as well. Upon closer inspection, one found in fact no complete résumé collected on any given page but rather piecemeal displays that introduced new elements each time and gave the impression of an inexhaustible abundance of positions and honors. He had written many articles, but no books; he mentioned a few volumes that were "forthcoming" and were likely to remain so. A single photograph was associated with his name on the internet, surprising for a person supposedly so prominent in the academic world. This photograph itself was enigmatic. It seemed to have been taken in the 1970s or, at the latest, at the beginning of the 1980s (whereas Barnett's publishing "career" had begun only in the 1990s) and the figure it depicted looked like a technician working for the FBI, a perfect supporting actor for a series like *The A-Team* or *Hawaii Five-O*.

At the time that he wrote to Charles, he claimed a double affiliation with the Centre National de la Recherche Scientifique in France and the University of Atlanta. It's easy to see this purported membership in two worlds as a principal key to his fraud. Etienne Barnett was an American scholar of French literature. The Americans must have been impressed by his French cachet (he even had a *baccalauréat*); the French must have been impressed by his American cachet. He could always pretend to be elsewhere, on the other side, to hide the fact that he was nowhere. He was a man of the Atlantic; his true place is perhaps on a Saint Pierre and Miquelon trawler, fishing the Grand Banks of Newfoundland.

He had given, as the location of his office at the CNRS (which has no record of him), the street address of the department store La Samaritaine. This little detail, among others, leads one to believe that he planned for the truth to be discovered someday, and that he sought to provide grist for the mill of those exegetes whose turn of mind was surely familiar by now, through his recopying of their texts. (As Charles remarks, you can find everything at La Samaritaine, everything and nothing.) In my opinion, he never set foot in the University of Atlanta, which he no doubt chose as a fictional base of operations—unafraid to give himself a lofty position in its administration—because he was sure that none of his peers or usual correspondents would have any contacts there whatsoever, and that this establishment itself might not have much occasion to come across his imposture. A quick internet search reveals that this University of Atlanta in no way resembles what we have in mind when we speak of the University of Poitiers or of Tübingen. The University of Atlanta is a private distance-learning institute founded in 1991; it doesn't appear to have a literature department.

No one has ever seen R.-L. Etienne Barnett. His web of influence must have woven itself solely through email correspondence; I bet he didn't use the telephone very often. He died by the internet, which was, however, the place of his existence, of the calls for papers he sent out, the recommendations he lavished upon others, without needing a body or a face.

Could he possibly have been unaware that it has become as easy to be caught copying as to copy? Some people are eager to make a martyr of him, a whistleblower, a figure of judgment—a person who does evil in order to denounce an evil greater than himself, who sacrifices his honor in order to cast discredit upon institutions or powers that be. They see him as the symptom of a debauched system whose logic he simply pushed to the uttermost limit. The quantitative evaluation of academic talent, become obsessive, encourages publications that merely serve to add a line to a résumé and that no one reads. Who, for that matter, could read them without wasting a life? Textual inflation is now close to exceeding the cognitive capacities of a human life span. Etienne Barnett is perhaps a victim—a victim of Shanghai Ranking. If he ever shows his face again, no doubt some good souls will help him to play such a role. This story gives a glimpse of a strange academic Wild West where microscopic campuses with pompous names spring from the ground between the saloon and the sheriff's office; where "publish or perish" is the first rule of a faithless, lawless world open to all brave souls itching to carve themselves out a little kingdom by any means necessary. Etienne Barnett is like that swindler on the bank of the Mississippi who passes himself off as Louis XVII, exiled far from France, in *Huckleberry Finn*.

The last word on this enigma has yet to be uttered, at the time of this writing. It is more or less certain that R.-L. Etienne Barnett doesn't exist, that no one bears this name or has held the positions attributed to him; that no Etienne Barnett has been concretely honored, celebrated, hired, or promoted thanks to this repeated plagiarism. The material advantages of this usurpation have, in the strict sense, profited no one. The person who hides behind this identity has only had the satisfaction of bringing into existence the character he or she has created: to see him cited, quoted, solicited, probably even courted. I lean toward a kind of American Jean-Claude Romand, someone who never finished his PhD, or who saw the doors of higher learning close in his face quite early, and who went on to pretend to belong to this world that had rejected him, all while inflicting tremendous humiliation upon its criteria of judgment, which are reputed to be so rigorous. I see it as a pariah's revenge, reflecting back the judgment upon those who once judged him.

Does this imposture have any pretensions to genius, as is often the case? In his plagiarized articles, the few interpolations in his own hand and the titles with which he rechristens the stolen texts are written in an imitative style, hopelessly jargon-filled, juggling notions of chaos, *dérive*, simulacra, etc. It's difficult to tell whether these express a naive faith in poststructuralism reduced to its most mawkish forms by a botched eternal student who believes this is indeed how it should be done and therefore endlessly mimics it; or whether it is rather a reductio ad absurdum—reminiscent of Sokal and Bricmont's modus operandi—of this very same poststructuralism with its subversive themes of the absent oeuvre, the death of the author, and the deconstruction of meaning, which over the past forty years have become an institutionalized refrain. Or it might even be a rather inventive application of these same themes in an ambitious forgery, a playful hoax in the manner—far debased, however—of Borges, Bourbaki, Marcel Duchamp, Raymond Roussel, or Vila-Matas.

The two latter hypotheses imply that the discovery of the hoax was an integral part of the project; it was meant to explode, like a kind of time bomb, amid the universal exhibition of texts in digital space. But by then it would be too late, the virus would already have spread, undermined the system, damaged reputations—the spider's eggs would already have hatched at various points around the web.

•

Agostino Ramelli, born around 1530 in Ponte Tresa on the shores of Lake Lugano, was an engineer and a soldier. It is said that he served in the armies of Charles V during the Italian Wars, but that didn't stop him from establishing himself in France a few years later, where he distinguished himself at the siege of La Rochelle under the command of the future King Henry III. During the latter's reign, Ramelli was in favor and received pensions and titles. It seems that in 1594 he sided with the League, against Henry IV, but later "Engineer Captain" Ramelli was again on the payrolls of the royal authority; he must have switched sides in time. He died at the end of the first decade of the 1600s. His biography has many gaps; in his own time, he remained obscure.

In 1588, in Paris, he published a work entitled *Le diverse et artificiose machine del capitano Agostino Ramelli dal Ponte della Tresa, ingegniero del christianissimo re di Francia et di Pollonia.* Except for the title page, all of the texts appear in both Italian and French. One-hundred ninety-five plates depict machines born of his imagination. They are complex assemblies of wheels, winches, and screws. Hydraulic power plays a large role. Ramelli seems to have been obsessed and endlessly inspired by a certain type of machine:

machines *to make water rise* using the force of the water itself—a combination of dams, wells, and waterwheels—compose about half of the illustrations. There are also movable bridges, catapults, machines for taking doors off their hinges or cracking strong locks.

Plate number 188 shows an invention that, in the context of the others, seems like an interlude, but which today has granted Ramello a legacy on an altogether different scale than the one reserved for him by time's tranquil progress in the years before the rise of the internet.

It's a book wheel; that's the name by which people have since come to refer to this object, though it doesn't figure in the chapter that describes it (Ramelli only says "this wheel"). It looks like a paddlewheel, a miniature Ferris wheel, or even the "wheel of fortune" that contestants had to spin on the television game show of the same name over twenty years ago (a highly anachronistic, even apparently burlesque comparison, but one which you can't help thinking of when you have the drawing before your eyes, and also one which fittingly evokes notions of luck, destiny, and games of chance). It is about as tall as a human. The user sits facing the edge, and the books, placed on tablets at a fixed angle, scroll past from top to bottom thanks to a highly sophisticated mechanism of epicycles activated by the user, in such a way that the works remain in place and are not at risk of falling. The user can, in this manner, browse through a dozen books. This invention is said to be not only "beautiful and artful" but also "exceedingly useful and convenient for all persons who delight in scholarship, principally those who are in poor fettle and subject to gout."

The ability to remain completely immobile is no doubt the only real advantage of such an apparatus, which otherwise seems impractical, slow, and even liable to provoke a fit of hysterics—simply imagine that you wish to compare two works placed on opposite sides of the wheel, and that you have to make repeated round trips by means of the crank that revolves this block of wood, which can't be very light. Surely a single table on which several volumes were conveniently spread out would fit the purpose as well or probably even better, with only one exception: it is indeed true that a scholar with painfully inflamed joints would sometimes have to rise, lean forward, and stretch forth his arm to handle the most distant volumes.

Ramelli no more built this machine than his dozens of baroque waterwheels. A few book wheels have been fabricated since then, nevertheless; they more or less resemble the model he established. In any case, it has become customary to credit him with the paternity of this invention—and to make of him, in the same stroke, a visionary precursor of hypertext links and the possibility of opening several windows on a single screen.

It's surprising that the human mind should be so eager to assign the most strangely convoluted and hapless precursors to its most brilliant and simplest creations. There is something touching about the way it attends to these awkward, stillborn first drafts and declares them to be its brothers, elevating them and at the same time gracing its own success with a halo of contingency and modesty. Such a paradox, in the realm of technical progress, perhaps brings us into the presence of what we would call, in the religious realm, a *mystery*. The inventors—without necessarily being able to explain it—are no doubt more sensitive to such a mystery than profane onlookers, and it would behoove us to respect this by refraining from jeering too loudly. So, if someone tells me that Ramelli's book wheel is a brilliant rough sketch of the internet, I agree to do my best to believe this, but only because it is absurd.

•

In April 1971, Michel Butor published an article in *Les Cahiers du Chemin* entitled "Remarks on the Book, Today." He announced the twilight of the codex, that "parallelepiped of printed paper" which threatens to be overwhelmed by the infinity of writing and whose superabundance it is becoming harder and harder to find space to store. "No matter how light it is in comparison to its ancestors, it is too heavy; no matter how abundant, too scarce; no matter how compact, too big." He then described, with surprising prescience, a few mutations to come, and that we have since witnessed: ubiquitous screen reading ("The advances in miniaturization [...] are such that it would pose no theoretical difficulty to condense the entirety of the documentation contained in all the world's libraries into a medium-size satellite; by means of a *reader* more or less resembling a television, anyone will able to consult any text at any time"); the end of editorial or space constraints as a limit to the publication of texts ("Everything, for that matter, will be able to be published, the satellites' capacities being easily vast enough to hold the totality of submitted manuscripts [regardless of what tool the hand uses to write them]"); the substitution of the number of consultations or views for the number of copies sold as the standard of success and profitability ("Complete overhauling of the bookstore, a new economy, and so new types of financing—royalties will no longer be a function of copies sold [there won't be any], but rather of consultations; a means of determining this quantity will have to be invented"); and finally, the augmented book, which we remain strangely slow to develop today, even though we have the means to do more or less everything that strikes us here as a relatively distant futuristic dream ("Current illustrations of a book on cinema only give us still images; if we wished, we could watch the whole shot; or for a book on music, our ears could hear each fragment of the score; in an art history book, each painting mentioned could be shown in detail; for foreign languages, at each word, we could have at our disposal an entire range of dictionaries automatically opened to the relevant entry; for a book on an author, we would have the entire context for each quotation").

Butor wrote these lines in the same years the internet was being born. But it would be completely anachronistic to see the slightest allusion to this in his remarks. The number of people who knew of the internet before the 1990s was minuscule, and rarer still must have been those who had even the slightest idea of all the functions and powers that it would constantly accumulate over the next twenty years—some of which seem prodigious in retrospect, when one makes the mental effort to place oneself in the precise circumstances of pre-digital life. The article doesn't even mention computers— neither the name nor the thing. It simply extrapolates from the potentialities that microfilm, televisions, satellites offered at the time. The imagination forges ahead in the certainty that, in any case, the technology department will follow its lead.

•

This certitude, in retrospect, expresses itself with stunning force in a very short text of Paul Valéry's, "The Conquest of Ubiquity," which dates back to 1928 and is cited more and more frequently today, because one finds in it certain phrases that seem to testify to a fairly considerable capacity for premonition, particularly this one: "Just as water, gas, and electricity are brought into our houses from far off to satisfy our needs in response to a minimal effort, so we shall be supplied with visual or auditory images, which will appear and disappear at a simple movement of the hand, hardly more than a sign." The material facts out of which he constructed his vision were the phonograph and the wireless telegraph.

This text's charm reminds me of a little black-and-white film from 1947 that I happened to discover when it was shared on social media. It seems to have already circulated extensively; it will continue to circulate, and probably widely, as it is a true curiosity piece. Its title is *Television, the Eye of Tomorrow*. It's a kind of science-fiction documentary, half playful, half serious, which imagines what daily life will be like in the future, thanks to technological advances. We see humanity equipped with portable individual screens that look a lot like our smartphones, in a barely larger size. People consult them while walking in the street; their posture is much like ours when we peer at our devices. When I saw this film for the first time, I thought it was a fake. After verification, it is cataloged and accessible on the website of the French National Audiovisual Institute. J. K. Raymond-Millet is credited as the director. The name René Barjavel also appears in the credits; he must have written the voice-over script, or at least significantly inspired it.

The projection extends further than the present moment and our current mobile phones. We see images escape from their devices and set themselves down everywhere, anarchically. A neighbor's television program passes through the wall, like the sound of a radio when the volume is too high; an excerpt from a film appears in a soup pot as the cover is lifted; an honest family man's sleep is disturbed by the three-dimensional apparition of a miniature bohemian girl dancing voluptuously on his bed.

Raymond-Millet's film, like Valéry's text, has been spared from oblivion because its prophecies have come to pass. Without the invention of the smartphone, these minor pieces would most likely have remained in the inmost depths of our archives. I probably wasn't alone in having completely forgotten that Walter Benjamin cites a long excerpt from "The Conquest of Ubiquity" as an epigraph to "The Work of Art in the Age of Mechanical Reproduction"—a text currently taught in all the universities of the world but which, ironically, might soon be replaced as an obligatory reference by Valéry's text, which has, until now, dwelt in the other's shadow. For that matter, even rediscovered, these pieces are still just as minor. They would remain so even if they became world famous. The capacity for prediction has never been one of the criteria for a masterpiece, and it isn't entirely unjust that the genre of science fiction, in which people place bets on the future, has almost always been considered minor. The pleasure that we experience in reading this text and in seeing this film may be traced to a reason that lies outside of them: the satisfaction of feeling that the gap between the imagination and technique is getting narrower, as if a plan of the mind were accomplishing itself before our eyes, with ever greater speed and efficiency, as if—a fairly new state of affairs, truth be told—we could live in the firm hope that everything which humanity has dreamed will come to pass; as if, at long last, the obliteration of the gap between dream and reality was breaking through on the horizon, like an incandescent, formidable point toward which our entire history will push us, when the hour of this extraordinary confrontation tolls.

•

When people in the year 2500 study the twenty or thirty years that preceded the revelation of the internet to the public at large around 1995, they will certainly be tempted to refer everything that was being thought and written at the time to this imminent event. It will seem as if we were expecting it, as if we already had a precise idea of it, as if we only had to wait patiently for a few moments while it was fine-tuned and delivered. This temptation will be even greater because the internet, at that time, did in fact exist in subterranean form. It takes a peculiar mental effort to force oneself to conceive that Butor, when he wrote the lines cited above, or Jacques Derrida, when he spoke of "the end of the book" in *Of Grammatology* in 1967, was absolutely unaware of the internet. What future historians will have to understand in order not to fall prey to retrospective illusions is that the apparition of the internet was truly a surprise, a breach in the flow of the passing years—and at the same time, that it came to fulfill an aspiration for which the imagination only possessed a very vague diagram, a faint sketch in dotted lines occupying the space opened up by the technological advances of the time.

•

"These automobiles.... I shall never get used to them..."

"How closely your thoughts concur with mine, Angèle."

"Do you think we shall soon cease to travel on horseback? Hubert, you who are informed of all such matters, you who are the minister's confidant, tell us..."

"Come now, dear friend, rest assured....How could we deprive ourselves of the tactile, living, cordial, even—I dare say—carnal, contact we have with this marvelous animal. Remember the words of Buffon.... The horse is the noblest conquest of man..."

"Nothing moves me so much as running my hand over the neck of a horse..."

"That is something unique... irreplaceable..."

"Horses have souls."

"Each horse has a story."

"Our bonds with them are so strong, so deep."

"The horse has been a pillar of our civilization for thousands of years..."

"Of every civilization, Edward.... Of every civilization..."

"You are right, dear friend.... A thing so deeply rooted in our mores will not disappear from one day to the next...."

"For my part, what I fear is that society will become even more unequal than it is today.... The rich who travel by automobile will be masters of speed—and hence of time—while the poor will have to make do with their old jades, their old broken-winded and obsolete carts."

"Rest assured, my dear... the minister is drafting a law that will oblige automobiles to drive no faster than horse-drawn vehicles."

"'Tis high time for such a law...."

"And when I think of all the farriers who are threatened with extinction if we do nothing.... They are the very soul of our villages..."

"And the coachmen... the carters..."

"So many employments lost... by the tens of thousands."

"And the oat growers, who will have no market, no clientele."

"It will be a catastrophe for French society."

"Have no fear, the State will help all such people to face this terrible crisis."

"Come now, my dear friends, the automobile has its merits as well..."

"Roland, we have hardly heard a word from you..."

"Tell us your opinion..."

"You speak seldom, but you often have the sharpest insight..."

"As each of you has so eloquently stated, the horse is inseparable from our lives.... Intrinsically so.... By its essence, I might say.... We shall always have need of the horse..."

"That is incontrovertible..."

"If even you agree..."

"But we must not reject en masse the contributions of Progress..."

"A wise observation, dear friend..."

"You are right.... So long as we contain the advances within reasonable limits..."

"Here, then, is my conviction..."

"Yes, Roland, tell us..."

"You whose lights have never failed you..."

"Well then....We shall always have a horse to run errands close to home, and we shall only use automobiles to travel long distances..."

•

Here is what a person could read in 1983, in the encyclopedia *Le cheval* by Jacques Sevestre and Nicole Agathe Rosier: "In the space of a single generation, the horse civilization has disappeared. A nearly universal civilization, the origins of which stretch back thousands of years, has just died without a murmur [...]. This is a decisive and irreversible rupture in the history of societies." If we replace the word *horse* with *paper* we obtain a fairly accurate description of the changes that have taken place since the year 2000—changes whose irreversibility we have been strangely slow to recognize, that we are even convinced we can and must resist, or that we spontaneously minimize by imagining the future to be merely a compromise with the present. Until, one day, we will stop for a moment, turn back, and realize that the thing whose necessity, whose eternal inalienability, we had proclaimed with such confidence has detached itself from us without a sound, and without our having noticed.

•

The comparison also suggests that books will never completely vanish, just as horses are still around, in equestrian clubs, where they are objects of aesthetic worship and enjoy a level of care whose technical precision verges upon a science. Books will undoubtedly meet with a similar fate, their sphere of existence limited and reserved—with all the advantages this entails—to leisure and art. They will also find themselves in the company of sailboats.

•

Another apocalypse: footnotes will vanish. They will be abolished and transfigured in an infinity of hypertext links, whose preliminary outline they have traced for a few centuries. A single text will be able to appear however we wish: at times traversed by millions of cross-references to other texts, to the world of things, to images and sounds, to botanical collections, grammars, atlases, to whatever we like, to all that we can unfurl from a single word, a single name, from the most enigmatic to the most trivial; and at other times naked and closed off, an interruption in the perpetual flow of things and meanings. Wave or particle, in a certain sense.

•

The Duke of Urbino—who, in the fifteenth century, amassed a gigantic library believed to have been the largest in Italy after that of the Vatican—has remained in the eyes of posterity the archetype of a conservative potentate indifferent to progress, the incarnation of technophobic snobbery, the symbol of luxury, of feudal scarcity disdaining democratic distribution, etc., because he allegedly made it a point of honor to keep only handwritten books in this library and refused even to lay eyes on a printed page.

This legend might be accurate, but it comes to us only through Vespasiano da Bisticci, who was the Duke of Urbino's supplier before becoming his biographer. Vespasiano was the largest bookseller in Florence; he counted among his clients the pope, the Medicis, and the King of Aragon. He was a fierce opponent of the printing press; to resist its advance, he attempted to elevate the production of manuscripts to an almost industrial scale by recruiting dozens of scribes. It was not a fair fight: he was forced to close shop around 1480. So he withdrew to write the lives of the illustrious men he had encountered in his time; and for his faithful patron who hadn't been seduced by rival innovations, he built a reputation that the latter was no longer around to correct.

•

One autumn evening, when night had just fallen, I lingered a little longer than usual before the stalls of the Boulinier bookstore on boulevard Saint-Michel. This was more than five years ago. Until that day, I had never realized that one could find so many books on sale for twenty cents apiece. At the time, if my memory isn't mistaken, the phenomenon of selling books on the internet at the price of 0.01 euros hadn't yet arisen. But even this made books one of the cheapest commodities in the world, less expensive than vending-machine coffee or individually wrapped cigarettes. And yet the consumption of a book, even a very short book, takes far longer than drinking a cup of coffee or smoking a cigarette. Regardless of whether it is poor or brilliant, the time required for the conception of a book is incommensurably greater; and, as Pliny the Elder used to say, no book is so bad that it can't be used somehow or other.

The absolutely heterogeneous nature of these dirt-cheap books was striking. For twenty cents, you could buy either *Le pari français* (The French Wager), by Michel Albert (Le Seuil, 1982, 398 pages), or a pamphlet ten times thinner containing the instructions to a household electrical appliance—but written in Czech. Neither the object's thickness, nor its nature, nor its quality (if any), nor the time it would take to read, nor the greater or lesser likelihood of its having any usefulness whatsoever seemed to have played the slightest part in fixing its price. There was no longer any value, because there were no longer any criteria of value. Even the "scrap prices" at which old freighters are sold couldn't be applied in the case of these books, for no distinction was made between the thickest and the thinnest.

Books had become a stock of goods that had to be immediately cleared out.

On the boulevard, an old orange Renault 5 drove past. These were the best-selling cars in France from the mid-1970s to the mid-1980s. They used to be everywhere during my childhood. You hardly see them anymore. Most of them were sent to the scrapyard. They weren't sold, not even for 0.01 euros. Their owners were given rebates so they would get rid of them and the cars would disappear. It's difficult to imagine that there might someday be a cash-for-clunkers program for books, but it's likely that many will be destroyed in the coming years for lack of buyers. Once a little time has passed—I said to myself that evening as I watched the car make its way toward the Seine—and those books that have remained untouched in attics reappear crowned with the halo of their newfound scarcity and the aura of things past, we will find them as charming as these old cars which used to be the very emblem of banality, and which we now turn our heads to look at when they mix with the traffic.

•

There are bookstores that have disappeared; others still will disappear. At least they will have been around long enough to intertwine their lives with the lives of several generations and to prolong their existence, as aesthetic images, in the memory—and melancholy—of those who frequented them at various stages. This privilege has not been accorded to those establishments that, at the turn of the present century, seemed at the vanguard of the new world and had in certain cases actually taken the place of bookstores (at the corner of rue

Soufflot and rue Le Goff, for example) or of old Modianesque bistros. It's already been a few years since the establishments I'm speaking of disappeared as quickly as they had arrived, as if punished for their over-hasty usurpation by their own premature and irrevocable ruin: we used to call them cybercafes. There were a few that I used to go to often, in the mid-2000s. I rarely remember that they existed, except when, in the course of a stroll, I come upon one of the storefronts that they had taken up with great fanfare and then stealthily deserted, without my having realized it, at a time when I, like so many others, no longer needed their services. Thus their brief existence is not altogether forgotten; it has passed into an intermediate state between total oblivion and that "great memory" which transfigures lost things and creates mythologies. Did one ever serve as the setting of a memorable film scene? Not that I know of. They are like those children who died before baptism, for whom medieval theology created the category of limbo, a foggy, barely determined notion, halfway between the hell they didn't deserve because they hadn't had time to do the slightest evil and the paradise from which they were excluded because they hadn't been absolved by the holy font of original sin.

•

The work of the translator can now rely on a new instrument that—unlike a traditional dictionary—doesn't define the meaning of words in one language by offering equivalents in another but rather by giving a whole series of images of the thing denoted by the word one seeks to understand. This iconological dictionary is called Google

Images. I think I used it for the first time in 2008—or at least that's when I first glimpsed its existence and power, with some astonishment—while I was translating into French a short story by Joseph Conrad that contained the following phrase: *belonging, as they did, to a warlike tribe with filed teeth.* . . . I asked myself what these "filed teeth" might be, and whether the phrase might harbor anything that a blindly literal translation, "*dents limés*," would miss. I typed the word into the search bar and saw a number of photographs of African warriors displaying sets of teeth in which the incisors had been chiseled into points.

Later, while translating Franz Hessel's chronicles of 1920s Paris, I spent a considerable amount of time—perhaps more than I spent flipping through my trusty old dictionary—searching on the internet for images of what he describes: mid-Lent parades, advertising posters of that era, old shop signs on the rue Mouffetard, remarkably ornamented facades, etc. I wanted to recover what the author had before his eyes; I wandered at length through the world to which the book referred. This way of doing things is more reassuring, more effective, and more pleasant than algebraic translation, which leads us from one word to another, without showing us the thing at hand. By seeing what the author saw, the translator takes another step toward this ideal: to put oneself in the place of the author, in order to rewrite the text in another language as if it had been written in it in the first place.

Some enigmas resist this, however. In an account by Walter Benjamin of a dream (which I didn't end up translating) I came upon the word *Fensterpult.* Benjamin visits Goethe's house, which strangely resembles a school with immense hallways; at the end of one of these hallways, he sees a golden book laid upon the *Fenster-pult*. My dictionary didn't know this compound word, which could be translated literally as "window desk." Indeed, that's how Jean Lacoste translated it at the end of the 1970s. But what's a window desk? Whether in French or in German, Google Images yielded no depiction of this bizarre piece of furniture, nor anything even close, not a hint that might point me in the right direction. The German word strangely called up photographs of the World Trade Center in flames; out of curiosity, I clicked on one of them, which carried me to an endless forum bristling with conspiracy theories. Nevertheless, I searched to see if the mysterious word indeed appeared somewhere, and I was led to an old image, taken from inside one of the towers, that showed a windowsill; this last was designated, in the attached description, as a *Fensterpult*. As I carried on with my inquiry, I saw that this definition had indeed been chosen by an English translator of Benjamin's, who proposed "window ledge" (another translator had preferred to skirt the difficulty by simply writing "desk"). Among very rare textual occurrences, a second hypothesis took shape, that of a "window table," a vitrine, in which objects are exhibited in a museum. This latter explanation is undoubtedly correct. The paradox—which postpones the hermeneutic resolution—is that we must imagine the golden book to be not *in* the window table but rather *on* it; for in the dream account, the warden of Goethe's house invites Benjamin and two elderly English tourists to sign their names on the open page—that's when Benjamin sees that his name is already there, in clumsy handwriting which is clearly that of a young child.

•

In another text of Benjamin's, which I translated in the spring of 2011, there was a statement attributed to the founder of *Le Figaro*, Hippolyte de Villemessant: "To my readers, an attic fire in the Latin Quarter is more important than a revolution in Madrid." As Benjamin quoted the phrase in German, I wanted to get my hands on the original French and reproduce it faithfully, instead of retranslating a translation. So I confidently set out to consult Google. But I noticed that every occurrence I found of this quotation came, either in an explicit or traceable way, from Benjamin's text. The good faith of the authors who repeated it wasn't in question, as none of them had any reason to doubt its authenticity; the phrase is plausible, and Benjamin has always been considered an authoritative scholar. If he disseminated an apocryphal remark, he undoubtedly did it in good faith. Perhaps he slightly altered the original statement; perhaps he himself had relied on a source that seemed certain, etc. I don't know how the enigma stands today. At the time, when I undertook this fruitless inquiry that always led me back to my starting point, I thought of that pair in *The Adventures of Tintin*, Dupond and Dupont, who find themselves driving in the desert and tracing a large circle around which they ceaselessly pass, convinced they are on a firmly established, well-traveled path, while they are in fact simply following their own ever more numerous tracks.

•

I hoped the internet would reveal the truth about a few enigmas from the final years of the pre-digital age about which I had read intriguing fragmentary accounts, or at least that it would provide me with new facts drawn from as wide a range of sources as possible, and so largely satisfy my desire to know more about these matters. The story of Jean-Paul Hütter is one of these enigmas. I had read of it more than fifteen years earlier in *Génération intellectuelle: khâgneux et normaliens dans l'entre-deux-guerres* (The Intellectual Generation: Khâgneux and Normaliens in the Interwar Period) by Jean-François Sirinelli, a voluminous historical work in which the life of Hütter occupies a few obscure pages constituting a veritable short story or sketch of a novel. The author has a good subject in hand, knows it, doesn't squander it; he treats it with a certain story-teller's talent.

Hütter was admitted to the École Normale Supérieure in 1926; on the entrance examination he was top of his class—*cacique*, as they say at the ENS. He was barely eighteen years old. This academic feat has few equivalents in the history of the institution. On the rue d'Ulm campus, he shared a room with three classmates: Albert Lautman, a philosopher, mathematician, and member of the Resistance, shot by the Nazis in 1944; Jean Maugüé, who taught philosophy in Brazil for many years and who, for some time after the war, served as the French consul in Thessaloniki and Toronto; and Dominique Leca, who passed the competitive examination for the Inspection des Finances in the early 1930s and found himself, in 1940, the chief of staff to Paul Reynaud, for whom he wrote remarkable speeches, as he also did later for several French presidents. In his memoirs, Valéry Giscard d'Estaing describes Leca as one of the greatest French speechwriters of the twentieth century, and he credits him in particular with the beautiful crepuscular speech in which Joseph Laniel announced before the dismayed National Assembly the defeat at Dien Bien Phu.

During *khâgne*—the second year of preparatory school for the ENS entrance exam—Hütter expressed sentiments favorable to communism; but in 1927 he put up two photos in a corner of the common room: one of Marshal Hindenburg and one of Adolf Hitler. In a memoir published in 1978, Leca recounted that Hütter commented upon these two portraits by saying, "Hindenburg is an idiot, but the other one is a prophet." Leca also recounted that it was on this day that he, Leca, heard the name of Hitler for the first time, from the mouth of his roommate. Maugüé—in his own autobiography published a few years after Leca's—also mentioned Hütter's premature conversion to National Socialist ideology. Other testimonies gathered by Sirinelli evoke the memory of a singularly "haughty" and "Nietzschean" young man.

Between the end of the 1920s and the end of the 1930s, Hütter wrote a master's thesis on the Westphalian cotton industry in the nineteenth century, passed the *agrégation d'histoire*—the national examination for history teachers—married a young German woman, sojourned in London and New York, taught at lycées in Lille and Strasbourg, and defended and published his doctoral thesis: "The Silver Currency Question in the United States, from Origins to 1900." He was mobilized during World War II and taken prisoner. We know that he was imprisoned at Oflag XVII-A, in Austria. From there, his trail strangely vanishes. It seems—according to information provided by Maugüé and Leca—that he was freed after only a few weeks, upon having sworn allegiance to the Nazis; that he was immediately named vice chancellor of the University of Strasbourg, which was again under German control; and that he then voluntarily enlisted to fight on the Russian front, in Wehrmacht uniform, and died there. But this story, which rounded out the black legend of the brilliant young man won over by the powers of darkness, was based on rumor rather than on positive fact.

An odd incident further deepened the mystery. Sirinelli remarked that the cross appended to Hütter's name in the alumni directory of the École Normale Supérieure had been omitted in the 1978 and subsequent editions, as if someone, or Hütter himself, had discreetly sought to indicate to the world that he wasn't dead, that he had simply disappeared and that he was, in one way or another, back in town. Alas, the elderly man who had overseen the printing of this directory for many years, and who could have explained this modification —it might have been merely an error or entirely incidental—died in 1982, before the historian Sirinelli was able to question him.

Sirinelli heard another version of the events from Hütter's younger brother, Roger Hütter, a graduate of the École Polytechnique and the former deputy director general of the French railway company (SNCF). Some of Jean-Paul Hütter's classmates at the École Normale—a circle dominated by progressive idealism—must indeed have been shocked by his taste for intellectual provocation, but he never in any way or at any time committed himself politically. In 1940, he was quickly freed only because his wife was German, and far from being named vice chancellor, he was demoted to a professorship much less prestigious than the one he had held before the war. He sent his relatives letters that expressed no pro-German sentiments, and rather hinted at the contrary feeling, whereas, knowing that his letters would be read by the censors, it would have been easy to exhibit his zeal to the authorities if he had given them his allegiance. In the autumn of 1943, he had been enlisted in the Wehrmacht against his will, and he died on the eastern front, in Courland, in 1944. His body was never found. The German authorities' report, seen by Roger Hütter, was not a death certificate per se; it recorded the testimony of two soldiers who had seen the French officer fall. Nevertheless, Roger Hütter didn't question his brother's death and didn't believe in a mysterious survival. Asked about the disappearance of the cross in the alumni directory, he claimed not to be aware of it. According to him, it must have been a misprint. He recounted to Sirinelli that, already at the end of the war, "allegations disseminated by a double agent" had sustained the idea that his brother had survived.

Long after having read this story and only just recently—I searched the internet hoping to find, if not a truth, then at least some additional information that might fill in a few parts of the puzzle. The very rare mentions of Jean-Paul Hütter's life on French sites come from Sirinelli's book. It is more disconcerting, however, to see his name resurface from the depths of human memory through the immense reference procedures with which we have now become familiar. Amazon invites you to order his book, based on his doctoral thesis. The systematic digitalization of academic journal archives of that time causes him to appear as the author of several articles and book reviews in the *Annales d'Histoire Économique et Sociale*. Some of them can be read in their entirety; glancing through these, I saw him sarcastically pointing out the errors his colleagues had committed in their works. One can also read two reviews of his book—one in French, the other in English.

The articles that one can track down are all—like Hütter's thesis —devoted to the history of, or current events in, the United States, and he had obviously become a specialist. It's curious, at first, to imagine a pro-Nazi scholar of American history, but then, it's far from impossible. His brother, for that matter, never invoked this

argument in his defense. There were many German literature scholars in the Resistance; one can be or become an enemy of one's subject
of study. (I see a distinction, nonetheless: an anti-Nazi scholar of
German history could tell himself that the real Germany, the Germany he loved, wasn't the one he had before him. It's much more
difficult to assert that the United States is anything other than what
it is.)

My very last search put me onto the trail of an American historian, James Friguglietti, a scholar of contemporary French history.
He apparently teaches at Montana State University. Another professor, John L. Harvey, cites him in a footnote to an article available
online, where he credits him with the revelation of Hütter's enlist-
ment in the German army. I was skeptical; I expected to find myself
in the presence of another "Dupond and Dupont in the Desert"
phenomenon, in which all new information would lead me back to
Sirinelli's book as its one true source, whether avowed or implicit.
This bold, to say the least, "credit" would probably turn out to be
the imprecision of a professor amicably citing his colleague without
being very familiar with the subject. I typed "Jean-Paul Hütter James
Friguglietti" into Google, and I came across a PDF of the program
of the fifty-third annual conference of the Society for French Studies,
held in Houston in 2007. Friguglietti was to deliver a lecture entitled
"Intellectual, Economic Historian, Academic and Traitor: The
Curious Career of Jean-Paul Hütter (1908–1951)."

Nineteen fifty-one! So a new chapter had yet to be written,
unless—and it wouldn't be the first time in the story—this was
another case of a misprint having slipped into the conference leaflet.
At a moment like this, one is inclined to light a cigar, even if only
an imaginary one, and settle comfortably into an armchair. I should

get in touch with Professor Friguglietti soon, I said to myself, as I drew puffs of smoke from my imaginary Havana cigar. Unless I wait for his paper to go up online, which is bound to happen one of these days.

•

Things that we will see no more. In the spring of 2003, I read in *Le Monde* a long portrait of Sacha Distel, a crooner from another era, whose past notoriety I was aware of, but nothing more. In this article, the author of which I have forgotten, there was a remarkable moment. Distel recalled that in the early 1950s, when he was barely twenty years old, he had played on Saint-Germain-des-Prés in an amateur jazz orchestra led by an extraordinary young musician, the best of their group he said, who was studying for the *agrégation* exam in philosophy. "His name was Hubert Damisch, I don't know what became of him." At this point, the journalist briefly abandoned his stance as an objective narrator—a fairly rare occurrence back then at *Le Monde*. He recounted his own surprise at this point in the interview and that he had explained to Distel that Damisch had become a highly esteemed philosopher and art historian—of whom I myself possessed a few books and who was, in fact, much better known to me than the famous singer. The two friends had gone their separate ways and carved out distant kingdoms for themselves, each unaware of the other. This formerly commonplace situation has become more or less impossible. It's no longer conceivable to go fifty years without looking on the internet to see what's become of those we still think of from time to time, even though we haven't seen them in ages.

A site which reposted this article—without giving the author's name—and which I've consulted today to shore up my memory, dates it to 2004. I'm certain, however, that I read it in 2003, in Montparnasse, in the apartment I lived in for a few months above the passageway that links the boulevard to rue Delambre.

•

The New Spirit of Capitalism, by Luc Boltanski and Ève Chiapello, was published in 1999, and the authors' preface states that the project began in early 1995. The term *internet* is nowhere to be found in the index to the French edition, which is understandable since—if I'm not mistaken—it indeed seems to appear only twice in the 843 pages of this voluminous work, and each time within a parenthesis as just another term in a list, for example in this phrase, on page 457, which refers to "the development of mail-order sales using all available media (telephone, post, the Internet) or of franchising networks, which mean that network heads do not have to bear the burden of all the assets."

I don't mean this as a malicious critique of this often brilliant book. Rather, I see it as a sign that the internet, when it became accessible to the public in 1995, at first appeared as a kind of improved Minitel, as one more object in the world's furnishings, and not as a new structure or new fabric of this world. It was toward the mid-2000s that the internet experienced its second birth; that people began to become aware of the profound changes it might bring to their existence; that it acquired the ontological significance, half real, half dreamed, whose sudden revelation impelled the project of these fragments.

This nearly total absence of the internet from *The New Spirit of Capitalism* is all the more remarkable in that the book describes with great precision the advent of a new "connectionist" world, in which the notion of the "network" becomes central—as it hadn't been, according to the authors, in the previous state of the spirit of capitalism, which was fundamentally bureaucratic. It's as if a moral revolution had preceded a technological revolution by a few years and, as it were, prepared the ground for it, or as if the moral revolution had, by some deeper causality, emanated from the gestation of a technological revolution that most people had yet to notice.

8

I HAVE THE IMPRESSION, when I look back on it, that my child-hood took place in an era of *the scarcity of images*. Such a character-ization would have seemed odd or even inconceivable at the time, for we already believed ourselves to be overwhelmed by a quantity of images never seen since the beginning of the world. And yet how rare they were in comparison to the overabundance we now have at our fingertips. We had to wait for them: wait for the films that were shown once on television and shown again only many years later; wait for the magazines that, once a month, brought a cargo of images that seems meager indeed, now that we can find on the internet, for every object and every desire, about as many images as we could wish. Images were a luxury that demanded patience. When we had one in our possession, we treasured it; we cut it out, pasted it into an album. From time to time, we went back to it and dreamily gazed at it for a long while. This relative scarcity of images had even made them into a kind of schoolyard currency—a currency now consid-erably devalued through overinflation. Today, images come one after another, devour each other, replace each other pitilessly, as if to outmatch the boundlessness of our desire.

•

PSYCHOPATHOLOGY OF DIGITAL LIFE, 4.—B. confides in me: "When I came into a little money, I thought I would finally buy myself some vintage watches, a country house, a 1970s Peugeot coupe. I looked at a lot of listings on eBay and leboncoin. I found a certain number of things that corresponded more or less exactly to what I had in mind. And I saw so many images of objects I desired that I became satiated. Fundamentally, I had found what I was looking for: images of these things, to my heart's content. Delving into my past, I realized that, for me, the ultimate goal of possessing an object had often been its aesthetic transfiguration into a series of images that represent it in its full glory, as at the office of my childhood doctor, whose walls were decorated with photographs of his yacht majestically leaning into the wind. I envied him; but today I tell myself that what I must have envied, at least as much as pure and simple ownership, was the fact that it could prolong itself in images, for images are the true place of aesthetic experience and pleasure. And so, since I had all the images I wanted, why subject myself to the—intermediate and tedious—stage of possession? In the end, I didn't buy any of it."

•

PSYCHOPATHOLOGY OF DIGITAL LIFE, 5.—Also from B., some time later: "I just got back from a long trip to Tunisia; I saw cities, shores, and ruins; I didn't take a single photograph. I told myself, more or less consciously, that I could find on Google Images as many representations as I liked of the places where I went, with an ease directly proportionate to the beauty of the place. I contemplated my digital camera, capable of taking photographs by the tens of thousands, and I told myself that it had become strangely useless, now that, thanks to its fellows, every image already existed. But I was glad to be fully present to the landscapes, without inflicting upon myself the photo sessions that had always—in my experience, at least—unpleasantly disturbed the fullness of these moments."

•

PSYCHOPATHOLOGY OF DIGITAL LIFE, 6.—From N.: "I take thousands of photographs; and since my storage capacity (though vast) isn't, strictly speaking, infinite, from time to time I have to make a few cuts. I generally start by sacrificing photographs that are poorly framed, those that my phone took without my knowledge, those that are blurry, those that once served as a mental note (photographs of book pages, Métro maps, etc.), those of objects I saw in shop-windows and thought I might want to buy later—in short, all the photographs that were taken without the least aesthetic intention and whose only function, most of the time, was to show something to someone or to keep a record of it for myself. Then I am overcome with a terrible doubt. Aren't these spontaneous images—these immediate, pure testimonies to a life and an epoch—the most important and even the most beautiful of all? Aren't they more valuable than the ones I took while pretending to be skilled in matters of framing or lighting, and proudly saying to myself, 'Ah! This will make a beautiful photo.' I tell myself that, twenty or forty years from now, these are probably the photographs that I will want to find, and that I will regret having lost if I destroy them today. I look at them again; they seem to me, in a certain way, the rudiments of a complete archive of the moments of our existence. Then these dust motes of my resurrection cry out to me to spare them, which, for a couple of days, I consent to do—until I get caught by the necessity of freeing up space on my phone, if I want to start taking photographs again."

•

There are so many images of everything nowadays that we have always already seen what we are about to see—be it an apartment for rent, the hotel in which we are going to spend a few nights for the holidays, the man we are supposed to meet for an interview, etc. Physical space is becoming the arena of a kind of general recognition where we go to meet up with images and verify what they have promised. More and more, we compare reality to images, instead of comparing images to reality.

Looking back to the 1980s or 1990s, I can't help thinking that we would have greeted this phenomenon as a miracle at the time— especially if it had arisen all at once, suddenly, and not in the course of a gradual process of technological evolution whose duration, though relatively brief, was sufficient to dull our capacity for astonishment.

The first time I visited the Greek island of Hydra, in August 2000, I don't think I had seen a single image of it beforehand, neither in a book, a newspaper, on television, nor anywhere else. I can't be completely sure of this, to tell the truth, but when I dig through my memory, I don't find anything that contradicts this total absence of preliminary images. The travel guide that I had back then contained no photographs; it offered only a basic map—a faulty one, for that matter—of the island. (I could have seen a fairly large photograph of the port with its village rising behind like an amphitheater in *Routes de Méditerranée* by Alain Grée, a sailing book published in the 1980s, but I only got hold of it one or two years after my visit.) It hardly matters. This uncertainty itself confirms my suspicion that I haven't greatly suffered from the loss of this experience of surprise, of pure discovery, of not knowing what to expect—a suspicion which, as I began to bring it to light and analyze it, immediately seemed firmly anchored in me and at the same time fairly odd, for we are accustomed to feeling wistful for the little frailties that made our prior condition more humble, more "authentic," and to being wary of the new powers that technology has granted us. Incidentally, I've never heard anyone else lament this loss, or even notice it, to tell you the truth.

The proliferation of images hasn't detracted from the singularity of reality, its force, its imprint. No matter how many hundreds of images we have of the place where we are heading, the fact of being there remains an experience that contains something entirely different—not unlike Kant's example of the hundred thalers, the concept of which is the same regardless of whether or not they are in my pocket, but the existence of which changes everything. Images, no matter how abundant, continue to create a desire for things, a desire for the coming into being of that which is imaged. This was already apparent in the pre-digital age, when things that had images were often more desirable than things unable or unwilling to display themselves.

•

When we used to miss an appointment with an image, we had very little chance of someday crossing paths with it again. Images weren't merely rare but ephemeral. Only a very small, elect circle had access to the Institut National de l'Audiovisuel. A person who missed the televised evening news on March 23, 1972, can now watch and rewatch it endlessly, if he wishes, as easily as the news of today, in the digital expanse that is the place of the integral resurrection—and exhibition—of images.

•

"The Artist of the Last Day," a prose poem by Yves Bonnefoy—published in 1987 in *Rue Traversière et autres récits en rêve*—evokes an imminent end of the world provoked by a kind of deluge of images. "The world was going to end suddenly because—a voice seemed to prophesy—in a few weeks, in a few days, perhaps in a few hours, the number of images produced by humanity would have surpassed the number of living creatures." Bonnefoy constructed an entire poetics—so articulated, ramified, and, as it were, systematic, that we could equally call it a philosophy—in which the notions of image, dream, illusion, and melancholy are attacked in the name of a quest for presence and simplicity. This text is one of the most beautiful instances of such a poetics; but the at least provisional defeat of the cause he championed has come to pass. The number of images has exceeded anything we could have imagined in 1987. The empire of the archive has planted its melancholy flag in the last bastions of the iconoclastic defenders of presence.

•

Leibniz stated the hypothesis of a "horizon of human knowledge" from which one can deduce the necessity of eternal return. He, as it were, toyed with this hypothesis without our being able to affirm that he made it his own. His reasoning was more or less as follows: Every event can give rise to a statement. And there exists a total number of statements that can be formed from the letters of the alphabet. No matter how large, such a number is well and truly finite, just as the staggering number of grains of sand in the desert is finite. In one text, Leibniz established the outer limit—the horizon—at $10^{73000000000000}$, below which must lie the exact number of all possible statements. A day will therefore arrive when everything has been said, when it will no longer be possible to say anything that hasn't already been said. Then, by virtue of the correspondence between deeds and words, no event will be able to take place that hasn't already occurred as well. The world will have exhausted its stock of events. It will end, and begin again.

•

This immense finitude can be glimpsed in the permanent accumulation of signs registered at every instant by the internet while the world goes on turning, a record in which one finds deposited, in the form of alphabetic statements, even the smallest mental or emotional events that rise to the consciousness of hundreds of millions of individuals.

•

In Guy Debord's *The Society of the Spectacle*, a critique of established political-economic systems—whether Soviet bureaucratic or liberal democratic—coexists with a pure philosophy, according to which the authenticity of life has to be reconquered in place of the images that have severed it from themselves. (Its fundamental premise bears an affinity with the thought of the Christian phenomenologist Michel Henry.) At the heart of this philosophy is a nostalgia for presence. "Everything that was directly experienced has withdrawn into a representation." The images that have detached themselves from life reconstitute themselves as a separate world, which life can only gaze upon by rending its own unity. Debord associates these two dimensions, the political and the metaphysical: behind the self-dispossession that existence suffers, a monopolistic power is at work, manipulating the spectacular in order to maintain and expand itself. The powerful impression created by his book lies in the convergence of these two dimensions. This, in a certain way, is what gives the book its timeless lyricism, its stylistic alchemy. It elevates to the highest degree the nature of these struggles whose final motto is: Negation of the spectacular negation of life; radical detachment from the world of detachment.

The internet has split apart these two dimensions. It has increased the flow of images that duplicate life, but it has given each individual the power to emit them, thus breaking up the great spectacular monopolies. Debord died in 1994, the year in which the first internet providers appeared in France. We shall forever regret the loss of the new "commentaries upon the society of the spectacle" that he would surely have devoted to this technology as he sought to determine to what extent it has overthrown the paradigm that his critical thought opposed (as one cannot but assume is the case).

As the spectacular monopolies were collapsing, the world of representation continued to expand while falling into disarray. Conspiracy theories were the first phase of a belief in liberty regained, the lever that toppled the transmission towers of institutional broad-casters. Debord spoke of the diffuse spectacle (liberal democratic) and the concentrated spectacle (Soviet). Perhaps we should invent the category of the esoteric spectacle (digital) in which life hands itself the mirror of a false reconciliation. In the concluding lines of his long preface to the Italian edition of *The Society of the Spectacle*—published in 1979, twelve years after the French edition—Debord seems to anticipate the atmosphere of a latent war whose theater is now the internet: "Under each result and under each project of an unfortunate and ridiculous present, we see inscribed the *Mene, Tekel, Upharsin* that announces the inevitable fall of all cities of illusion. The days of this society are numbered; its reasons and its merits have been weighed in the balance and have been found wanting; its inhabitants are divided into two sides, one of which wants this society to disappear." This writing on the wall shows through in the insults directed each day at traditional media, vestiges of the diffuse spectacle descended into the digital arena. But the struggles unfolding before our eyes hardly seem to portend life's victory over representation. The partisans of pure criticism are so persuaded of being in direct contact with the truth that they do not see the new illusion into which they have shut themselves. We have no dialectic by which to set these incomplete figures back into their place.

It's hard to tell if Debord would have detected emancipatory virtues in the internet or if he would have seen it as a new form of spectacle. One might surmise that his fundamental metaphysical thesis would incline him toward the latter. This thesis is so radical that it is essentially inalterable. For, since the beginning, everything that was directly experienced has withdrawn—into a memory. In a

philosophy of recollection—or of the internet as an immense recollection machine—life reunites with itself only in the separate
world of memories, melancholically.

•

One Sunday afternoon, in November 2012, I went for a walk along
the banks of the Seine; I hadn't done so for some time. I slowed my
pace, as usual, at the stalls of the secondhand booksellers. Many of
them sell old postcards; I had never taken much interest in these
goods, even though I've always enjoyed getting books there. Stopping at random, I absentmindedly began to flip through a box that
seemed to contain pretty cards; they were placed directly on the
parapet, right next to the stall, as these boxes generally are. I ended
up spending a long while looking at these postcards. I contemplated
their strangeness. I had forgotten how familiar this object used to
be in times past; I hadn't fathomed to what extent it had become
exotic, to what extent it had fallen into the distant past. I flipped
them over; most of them had served their purpose, been sent. I instantly
rediscovered the handful of ready-made phrases we used to write
on them out of habit—the weather is lovely here; the water's just
right for swimming; thinking of you very fondly—often embel-
lished, at the end, with a few words added by the awkward hands of
one or several children. I, too, had once been made to write these
little postscripts. How could I have so radically forgotten the existence of postcards? What had replaced them? Did eight-year-old
children now send text messages to their grandparents—or photo
messages of their sandcastles? The photographs in these two or
three boxes all depicted landscapes. The postcard, I told myself,

must have been—initially and, so to speak, intrinsically—a *landscape shot*; for its purpose was to show the recipient what the sender had before his eyes, what surrounded him. That's why this object—independent from the advent of its technical feasibility—had acquired its full significance through the establishment of the colonial world and, later, the democratization of vacations. I was struck by the number of postcards from the 1950s or 1960s proudly displaying shots of large modernist blocks of concrete that we would deem ugly today, or at least ill-suited to serve as advertising symbols. (Jacques Tati mocks this characteristic feature of the era in *Trafic*, by dotting the film decor with travel agency posters boasting of ever more exotic destinations, but always displaying the same large parallelepipedal glass-and-steel building.) Humanity, proud of its creations and of its progress, had exhibited itself, sent itself images of the large rational buildings it had summoned from the earth, triumphing over chaos and shortage. I reflected that such a close link with the tastes of the age had signed this object's death warrant; I bought a dozen of them.

In paragraph 14 of *Discourse on Metaphysics*, Leibniz writes that God "turns, so to say, on all sides and in all fashions, the general system of phenomena which he finds it good to produce for the sake of manifesting his glory, and . . . regards all the aspects of the world in all possible manners." This figure has often merged in my mind with the image of a person turning 180 degrees, first in one direction and then the other, one of those rotating postcard stands that we used to see at the entrances to newspaper kiosks at seaside resorts. I no longer remember whether I invented this analogy, or if it was one of our *khâgne* professors, Jean-Louis Poirier, who caught our attention by using it during one of his lessons on Leibniz; he would have been capable of it, and the mere fact that I have a doubt leads me to believe that I do owe it to him. It came back to mind as I was skimming through these boxes of postcards, whose primitive monadology seemed suddenly accomplished, augmented—but at the same time swallowed whole—by the infinite picture gallery of Google Images.

•

About fifteen years ago, as I was walking alone in a place I found extraordinarily beautiful, I had a pang of regret that no one was there to share these aesthetic experiences with me. But I didn't regret my solitude; it was one of the conditions of the intensity of such moments. Rather, I would have wanted that impossible thing: solitude and, simultaneously, the immediate communication of what solitude made me witness. I remember having fervently wished to overcome this contradiction one day in April 2000 on the Île d'Ouessant—at a time when cell phones were still only used for making calls, and I didn't have one anyway. I was following the path that runs along the southern end of the Baie de Lampaul and leads the ambler from revelation to revelation, from the Saint-Guénolé washhouse (a perfect arrangement of water, stones, and thick grass, a little open-air theater scene surely inhabited by invisible sprites ceaselessly playing *A Midsummer Night's Dream* above the sea) to the cove whose perfect circle seems to have been drawn by the finger of some geometer god, right next to the point that reaches into the ocean to enclose the bay. Years later, in 2013, in London, I took a series of photos with my phone in the Barbican water gardens, in the encroaching twilight, and for whatever reason, precisely at that instant, I had the feeling of truly understanding what it means to be able to immediately "share" with "friends" the photographs of the places in which we find ourselves. The contradiction between solitude, as a condition of aesthetic experience, and communication, as the intimate aim of this experience, was suddenly resolved with an efficacy that, a few years earlier, would have seemed unimaginable. I looked at my camera; I nearly pushed the "share" button, as if this had become an obvious, natural, even necessary gesture; and I held back my finger.

•

Returning from a brief trip to New York, in June 2014, I had to wait several hours before boarding. This was at Newark airport; through the bay windows, you could see planes taking off one after another at brief intervals. I was reading the last pages of Susan Sontag's *On Photography*. I had started it four years earlier in London, where I had bought it at a bookstall on Brick Lane; taken it up again in Greece in the summer of 2011; and then forgotten to finish it. And yet I liked it very much. I had remembered it again before leaving and thought it would make good company for a trip to America. I also had the intuition that it might prove inspirational for the texts on the internet that I was writing. When I closed the book, I still had a lot of time ahead of me. So I reopened it and started reading it again, from page one.

At several points in the first chapter, Sontag speaks of tourists, a subject of particular interest to me. Many of them, she says, feel obliged to place the camera between themselves and the remarkable things that they meet on their way, as if to calm the disorientation their distant journeys had brought on. The book dates to 1977. I was reminded of what B. had told me, of the exasperation he felt at the camera's intrusion into his experiences of the splendid sites he visited. This feeling, to tell the truth, wasn't foreign to me; I too, during the age of film photography, had sometimes returned from a trip with only a few snapshots, or none, because I hadn't wanted to deprive myself of a full, undivided, unobstructed presence.

But it seemed to me that things had changed from the time when you had to stick one eye to the camera—closing the other—while you took a photograph, an act that clearly and even brutally cut you off from present experience and its unbounded enjoyment. Now, tourists used tablets which they held at arm's length, even farther away than the smartphones and early digital cameras that had first freed the human eye from the photography machine. These tablets were often protected by a case that folded over them like a book cover; and so it was common to see, during those years, while paper was threatened with extinction, people lifting their arms to the sky to brandish books they seemed to be reading from afar. That morning, before heading to the airport, we had boarded a tour boat for a sightseeing cruise around Manhattan. In front of the Statue of Liberty (who, at present, herself seemed to be holding a tablet in her left hand) we had all stretched out our arms, myself included. One could now see the image at the same moment as the reality it represented; the landscape, at the same time as its photograph. And yet, this didn't restore the fullness of experience. The eyes swung between the screen and the world, which had now become a background to which one could attempt to return by looking away from the machine, but only at the risk of taking crooked, botched, useless images—and so the old dilemma had returned: to see or to photograph, to enjoy the present moment or to build a stock of memories.

What had also changed, of course, was that one no longer had to wait for the shot to be developed, which used to take a few days or a few weeks. Now, one could not only see the general effect but also immediately compare the image with the reality. When I got my first smartphone, I remember having been disappointed precisely because the image was never true to reality, the proportions and distances were too distorted, and so, for a while, I balked at using the magical power to take photographs by the thousands that this new camera had granted me. Later, I came to my senses. Analog photographs also used to distort space, but since we received them after a delay, without being able to compare them with the original scene, we were less shocked; and I realized that one forgets a digital photograph's lack of fidelity when, after a little while, one is simply glad to recover its testimony of what took place. Once reality disappears, we're grateful that the image exists. We no longer worry about gauging its fidelity; we no longer can.

As I daydreamed about the future of the touristic condition and, from time to time, watched the airplanes take off, I continued to read Sontag: "After the event has ended, the picture will still exist, conferring on the event a kind of immortality (and importance) it would never otherwise have enjoyed." Shortly after falling upon this sentence, I set the book down at my side, thought for a moment about something that had been running through my mind without taking definite shape until that instant, and picked up my phone. But instead of taking a photograph, I began to record a video. Holding the device firmly against my seat's armrest in the waiting room, I aimed it at the window and, for three minutes, filmed the merry-go-round of trucks in the foreground and, a little beyond, the airliners taking off. Then, by immediately watching this record-ing, I played at stopping the progression of time. I raised the device and tried to block out the large window with my minuscule screen on which there streamed a spectacle very similar in appearance to present reality—it was always planes and trucks, new ones that were the same—but ontologically very different, for it was the past, a past that resisted, that didn't want to leave, that came back and clung to the present, doing its best to supplant it. I fell under my own spell; I suspended my disbelief, as Coleridge says of the reader of fiction; I pretended to convince myself that the manipulation of time was almost within reach.

I thought of all those situations when, as a child, one is forced to wait, to wait for a very long time, while watching repetitive phe-nomena—for example, in the backseat during endless vacation trips—and one invents solitary, mechanical games, bordering on what contemporary psychology calls "obsessive-compulsive disor-der." Perhaps children confined to family cars will start filming clouds or highway trucks, and play at stopping the progression of time, constantly repeating the same scene and superimposing it upon the present—as if to abolish or kill time that never ends, as if to imagine themselves deities and forget the passive state in which they are locked.

•

PSYCHOPATHOLOGY OF DIGITAL LIFE, 7.—F. confides in me: "Until the 2000s, I watched a lot of television. I didn't particularly enjoy it; in hindsight, I think I mostly turned it on out of weakness;

and then I would have a very difficult time turning it off. The things streaming before my eyes often seemed idiotic; and yet I watched them, fascinated by their emptiness. Do you remember the letters-to-the-editor segment in *Télérama* or the radio-television supplement of *Le Monde*? Each week, there would be at least one or two letters railing against the haplessness of the programs, and you couldn't help thinking that if you were ever face-to-face with these letter-writing grinches, you would tell them that, after all, no one is obliged to watch television, and if they didn't like it then all they had to do was turn it off. Personally, I understood them; it was more complicated than that; it wasn't so easy to fight the need to watch the damn television. It was like cigarettes. I often told myself: Tomorrow, I'll quit. And then I would start again. Now, I never watch television anymore. I had a fairly old set that became obsolete and unusable after the switch to digital television, in 2011, I believe; I took the opportunity to cut myself off. But a little while later, I fell into the internet; it was a different kind of addiction, but it had many points in common with the previous one. Once I had turned on my computer, I'd spend hours clicking from link to link, launching the most unexpected Google searches, which would arise from the previous steps of my wanderings, according to a more or less logical progression of ideas. I managed to justify my extended journeys in this spiral by persuading myself that brilliant ideas or ultimate mysteries might well be revealed to me, someday, from the depths of the internet, in hidden digital realms where I would be the only one to have ventured. It's surely no coincidence that the notion of *serendipity* spread considerably during the early 2000s, in parallel with the internet. That word must have come to the aid of many a casuistic defense, it must have put to rest many a scruple of conscience provoked by this new way of wasting time. Often, I emerged from my explorations almost as empty and disgusted with myself as I used to be at the end of a long afternoon spent in front of the television in years past. There were times I couldn't bring myself to leave the house, saying, 'All right, one more search, a last search'—like an alcoholic who promises himself that the next glass will be the last—and then I would keep doing search after search until night had fallen and it had become absurd to go anywhere at all. In the age of television, I had the impression that society was forcing its obsessions upon me, and I reproached myself for not putting up stronger resistance; now, while believing myself to be freer, I lock myself up as much as I please in my own obsessions, and I'm starting to wonder if this isn't more dangerous."

•

PSYCHOPATHOLOGY OF DIGITAL LIFE, 8.—From the same, a little later: "Come to think of it, have you heard anything about television lately? It's dying, isn't it? Unless it's already dead. I wouldn't know, I'm not interested in it anymore. Maybe I'm like the old hermit that Zarathustra passes coming down from his mountain who doesn't yet know that God is dead. When I say dead, I mean in the form we knew of it in the 1980s and 1990s. That was its quintessential state. It had entered into every household; it had invaded our existences and minds. The *intellectuals* were alarmed. *Channel surfing* was a threat to civilization. The average human no longer aspired to anything more than pushing the buttons of a *remote control*, a supremely nonchalant gesture which, in the eyes of moralists, signaled the abolition of all intellectual effort, the victory of laziness and disdain. We had become incapable of understanding, respecting, and shouldering the austere grandeur of our heritage; we watched *Japanese animé* in the afternoon and *variety shows* in the evening. Television completed and symbolized the hegemony of an empty present. The past was hidden, scorned, ridiculed; it was the realm of such fusty old things as black-and-white and text, things that no one cared about anymore and that were banished from the broadcast channels without the least scruple. The internet has rung in the revenge of the archive and sounded the death knell of the *show*, which used to set the beat for the triumphal march of the present. It has also erased the differences that used to exist between different forms of media. The television as we knew it has been condemned to death by drowning, in this dissolution of boundaries. Radio, television, and newspapers no longer exist; there are neither monthlies nor weeklies. There are sites that offer text, images, and sound, and that constantly update the news they publish. As for the two or three remote controls I still have from the 1990s, they've been gathering dust for years. I can't even remember which one was for the *television set*, which for the *videocassette recorder*, which for the *hi-fi stereo system*, and so on. They all look the same. Besides, I never knew what most of the countless buttons on the keypad were for. The "'Boeing control panel' aesthetic that characterized those ancient times has sunk into oblivion; it has been replaced by the naked whiteness of the Google home page, and the kingly gesture no longer consists in commanding something from afar but in touching your finger to a screen. Devices have come closer to our bodies; all that remains is for them to cross the threshold and enter the intimacy of our minds."

•

People's astonishment when, in times past, they would meet a movie star and find her "nicer in person" than on-screen will soon be experienced when we meet more or less anyone—all those whose traces or representations we see on the internet before we meet them in the flesh.

•

Perhaps there will come a time when we direct films starring long-dead actors for whom we have reconstructed deceptively exact avatars, based on their former performances. Ten years ago, I imagined a Hollywood adaptation of Plato's *Symposium*, in which Socrates would be played by Orson Welles and Alcibiades by Marlon Brando.

•

In a recent dream, I was looking at images on the screen of a smartphone and, little by little, without my being surprised or even noticing anything unusual (as is often the case in dreams, where changes of place and condition come one after another and multiply as if naturally), these images escaped from their technological medium; they no longer needed a device to project themselves on the walls, the ground, anywhere they pleased, even *on nothing*—in the air, haphazardly tiny or gigantic, free of all measure or law, like mental images having exteriorized themselves as they anarchically strewed themselves along my path.

•

In 2009, there was a possibility that I might teach philosophy and literature in Tunis. Nothing came of it, but it occupied me every now and then and seeded a few daydreams over the course of several months. At that time, I had a dream in which I had in fact settled there. As I had never visited in real life, the dream images didn't have much material to work with; the geography of the site was extremely simple. I had a little apartment; I remember that down below at the edge of the sea there was a ledge along which I could see myself walking from time to time, as if along the path I routinely took to the university (though I haven't retained any image of the latter, or of myself at work; it must have been before classes started), or else to shop for groceries, or simply to go for a stroll. This was more or less the entire universe of the dream, for its time frame was brief— three, four, maybe five days—and, as will be seen, we can suppose that my stay didn't extend any further. Tunisia was ruled at the time by Ben Ali, a dictator who seemed eternal, and who in early 2011 would be overthrown. My apartment had a kind of rudimentary but pleasant living room, principally furnished with a sofa and a coffee table. That's where I see myself most often; and in this living room, of course, there hung a portrait of Ben Ali.

I don't know anymore if it was on the day I arrived or, more likely, the following day, that I was seized with a whim to cover this portrait with a portrait of Mao (which I pulled out of my luggage or pocket like a rabbit out of a hat), to ridicule the cult of personality that surrounded the local despot; at least that's how I have pieced together the main motive of this gratuitous, imprudent, sardonic, and brash gesture that is not very much in keeping with my general disposition. At the time, I was far from imagining that a few years later I would write a fictional story whose plot centers on an episode of the Cultural Revolution and whose cover shows a portrait of Mao hanging on a wall above a desk.

A day passed. I think I was returning from a walk along the ledge; I was in the living room again. My telephone, lying on the coffee table, spontaneously lit up, as if summoning me. I opened it—one of those flip-phone models that are now obsolete—and I saw a video that showed me performing the insolent deed of the previous day. The device had filmed me without my knowledge, as if by magic. I panicked. The next day, I walked along the ledge again, uncertain of what would happen to me now. The rest is a muddle; I only remember being in my bed, suddenly surrounded—or, I should say, covered—by prostitutes who had entered from I don't know where, since all I could see was their pleasant tangle of limbs; I knew that my fate was sealed, that my telephone, though still lying in the next room on the cursed coffee table, wouldn't miss a thing; and then the idea of a last revel swallowed all fear and care for consequences, I said to myself something like *Full speed ahead!* and I woke up.

•

For the Scholastics, the angels were a kind of experimental being endowed with the perfections that humanity judged itself to lack. These hypotheses, or, so to speak, these fictions, revealed all sorts of difficulties, paradoxes, or impasses, on a moral or metaphysical level, which gave rise to endless controversies that we would be wrong to continue to ridicule too much today, not only because they often have a real literary merit but also and above all because we—who have come face-to-face with our own perfection—can find questions there that resonate with our own situation, present or future, and that are paradoxically more relevant to us than they were to the men of the Middle Ages who formulated them.

I'm not well versed enough in theology to know if anyone has ever attributed to angels the ability to see themselves from without as others see them. (Perhaps the question never arises, since angels don't have bodies; or perhaps it does arise, precisely for that reason.) It's easy in any case to see this as something that is missing from our experience, a faculty our condition lacks. I remember how strange I felt the first time I used Skype. What troubled me wasn't the image of my interlocutor speaking to me from the other end of the earth— after all, science fiction had so long familiarized us with this dream of the videoconference that it didn't affect us much when it became possible. What troubled me was the other image, the little image at the bottom right, where I saw myself speaking; and even more specifically, what troubled me was the vague presentiment I had of witnessing, in this splitting of perception, something that would one day become a permanent and, as it were, commonplace element of our existence.

In fact, all it takes to make this daydream concrete is to imagine that ultra-miniaturized drones accompany us at every moment, transmitting images of us to a Google Glass–type device, or better yet, in a slightly more distant future, transmitting them to the post-digital internet within our minds to which we would have access—without any exterior device—by a pure act of spirit.

•

Near where I live, there is an Italian restaurant where I have been a regular for a fairly long time. Reproductions of vintage cinema posters hang on the walls; one is of a 1960s James Bond film starring Sean Connery. I've seen this poster dozens of times, and I don't know why it particularly caught my attention one night and became the source of a curious intuition. The picture of the young Sean Connery clashed in my mind with the image of him in his later years. I thought of those pages on Google Images where you see the photographs of great actors from the olden days as they were at the height of their glory, side by side and almost in conflict with the images of them as they are now, changed by the years and, sometimes even more horribly, by the vain battles they have sought to wage against these years. My daydream continued and brought an old reflection to the surface. When I was twenty, I asked myself—naively and cruelly—how people could bear to see their reflections in the mirror once they had grown old. Later, I felt that I had found the answer, when I saw myself suddenly grown old in photographs, even though, each morning, I didn't particularly feel as though I had changed: in a mirror, we never see ourselves as we are; we see ourselves as we have been. Years of looking in the mirror come between us and our sight—by a kind of phenomenon of retinal persistence —and distort the image in our favor. Photographs, however, aren't so charitable; they sweep aside the fragile lines of defense much as they show in a stark light the poor cut of an outfit that we, by a thousand little shifts before the mirror, had pretended to find properly tailored. The same phenomenon masks the physical change of friends we see every day, while those we meet again years later appear horribly disfigured by time. (I have often thought that the narrator of *In Search of Lost Time* succumbs to this illusion when, at the very end of the book, he meets up with his old fashionable society friends and describes them as unrecognizable ruins, all while remaining convinced that he himself has hardly changed at all, abetted in this by his interlocutors who feign astonishment at finding him still looking so young—and for once, he doesn't trouble himself to uncover the egregious formality of their words which, for that matter, it never crosses his mind to reciprocate.) This association of ideas led me to the vague vision of a future time when the proliferation of liberated images, untethered from any fixed ground, will have become so vast that these images will allow us to control and alter our appearances. Surgical modification of reality will have become pointless; ugliness and old age will be hidden behind infinite images. *Intentional species*, those "little images flitting through the air" scorned by Descartes and the majority of eighteenth-century philosophers, will thus gain, in an unexpected way, the reality that was so vigorously denied them. Objects will emit images of themselves, images which more or less resemble them and which will be the only thing we perceive of them, in accordance with the intuition that Lucretius first expressed in antiquity and that persisted through Scholasticism, until the advent of modernity.

9

CHRYSOSTOM LANGUISHES, for no Wikipedia page exalts his name. And yet his genius has embraced Metaphysics, Mathematics, and Poetics; he also plays the organ. He has published, at his own cost, works still concealed from the notice of the world—whether some accident in the progress of the human spirit obstructs their coming to this wider light, or some wicked cabal conspires to occlude his own renown, which could not otherwise have failed to flourish. This page one day appears, created by a user who gives his name as *Theophrastus*; soon thereafter, the page is translated into fifteen tongues, among which are *Suomi* and *Esperanto*. Theophrastus withholds no praise an author dreams of, and we learn that in his twelfth year, Chrysostom's tutors considered him to be one of the kingdom's most precocious geniuses. When scholars read this, they marvel at never having heard the name of one endowed with such great merit; they inquire of booksellers, newsmongers, members of the Academy, and the finest wits at court: not one can say who this Chrysotom is. Two Wikipedia moderators, *Philalèthe* and *Epaminondas*, after brief inquiry, suspect that Theophrastus and Chrysostom are one and the same person, who has fabricated his renown, cloth and stitch; they hold that this page should be removed, and submit their proposition to debate. Chrysostom appears and defends himself; he addresses them in these words: "I am told, kind sirs, that a quarrel has here arisen, of which I am the object. I who live far retired from the world, who hardly know how to use a *computator*, who until this sinister day was unaware of the existence of your encyclopedia, how could I have formed the least notion of these stratagems you lay at my door? Let vulgar souls pretend to glory; I aspire to truth alone, and I live in such abnegation and obscurity as she requires of all her humble adepts. I have died a thousand deaths upon learning of these accusations, which paint a picture of me so far removed from my own true self, that I assure you, I would that I had never appeared in your encyclopedia at all." Philalèthe and Epaminondas pretend to recognize a man of good sense, and desire to prevent his subjection to further embarrassment: "If indeed, Chrysostom, you are in no wise the author of this page, you must take up your guard against the wicked prankster who has done you this mischief by creating it. Merely say the word, and we shall remove this entry." To which Chrysostom promptly replies: "You know as well as I, kind sirs, that works of the spirit live independent of their authors, in proportion as they delight their audience. What am I to do if a few readers, in good faith, surprised, by all appearances, to find my work's modest influence still enclosed in such deep silence, see fit to do me homage? I am so little acquainted with these persons, how could I keep them from sowing a few errors in the tale they tell of my life. How could I have created my own page, I who cannot even correct the least word of what is said of me on your machines?" Two of Chrysostom's zealous admirers, *Théagène* and *Euphorion*, of whom nothing more is known, enter the fray; and they seem so thoroughly to have imbibed Chrysostom's works, that they write in the same grandiloquent style as he. "That Chrysostom be unknown to you, does not therefore argue him unknown to all. We may attest to his fame in our city of *Burdigala*. The illustrious *Roscius*, a correspondent of the Institute, recently and in our presence praised his work on the corruption of taste in the present century, etc. What has he done to merit such slander from your tongues? Is it jealousy that masters you, Philalèthe, you who have never penned a single book? Would you add insolence to irrelevance, Epaminondas, by denying a worthy man the fame which has fled your person?" Finally, two subjects of the English crown appear, *Melchior* and *Julius*, of Oxford, who converse in schoolboy Latin; they pretend that Chrysostom's renown is manifest, and submit that his commentaries on Corneille's tragedies, though less celebrated than those he produced on Racine's, might yet be greater still. Philalèthe, after a brief time, deletes the Wikipedia page which relates the life of Chrysostom. The latter protests once more, complains of libel, asks why the entire world so obstinately seeks his ruin. "I, who know nothing of how a computator works, etc." He is not entirely wrong; clearly he does not know of such a thing as an *IP address*. Philalèthe, who does, has observed that every tirade of these many characters has issued from the selfsame author: Chrysostom.

•

Theognis is greatly active on the *Universal Book of Faces*; he posts each day many photographs of himself, dressed by the kingdom's finest tailors, smoking cigars imported from the West Indies, his eyes concealed behind those *tenebrous glasses* actors most in favor affect to wear, to escape the notice of passersby. Who could imagine but that he goes from coach to coach, palace to palace, ceremony to ceremony, and is the bosom friend of great lords, several of whom are seen photographed in his company. He knows the life of the court better than it knows itself. He wittily comments upon the fall from grace of each duke, minister, or cardinal. People ask him of the passions of princesses, the dallyings of favorites, the marriages of ladies-in-waiting. Theognis is nineteen years old, has no estate, and lives in a garret. He has a knack for slipping into parties to which he has not been invited, and for retouching photographs.

His deceit, unmasked, merely augments his fame. He justifies himself, not without eloquence: "I obeyed the maxim of Monsieur de La Rochefoucauld, who says that *to establish ourselves in the world, we must do all we can to appear established.*" A handful of repartees of this sort are enough to make of him a fashionable figure; people seek him out, repeat his witticisms, share the sayings he lavishes upon his *followers*. He becomes one of the most *viewed* figures in the digital expanse. He has four footmen, one hundred thousand followers, two hundred fifty thousand search results on Google, and a more than reasonable number of friends on the Book of Faces. The Duke of C—— takes him under his protection. This is how, in failing to feign to be what he was not, he became it indeed.

•

Menippus knows that *Orante* was yesterday in *Novum Eboracum*; that *Titus* sojourned several days in *Ebuses* along the shores of the sea; and that *Lycaon* is returned from *Berolinum*, where he delivered a lecture. Nothing of what happened to them in these lands escapes Menippus's eye. So vast is his knowledge, he tries at times to feign ignorance. "And what about you, Menippus?" Titus asks. "Where were you during this time?"

"I know," says Orante, "Menippus was at his computer, voyaging on the Book of Faces."

•

Alceste, under the pseudonym *Geronte71*, daily chastises the turpitude of senators, on the sites of *La Gazette* and *Le Mercure*: they neglect the public good, purchase their idleness through exorbitant taxes, and have not the least particle of the spirit and taste they claim to hold. He is especially wrathful toward *Archytas*, the Marquis of B——, whom his imagination pictures in the likeness of *Sardanapalus*. "Would to God cruel Archytas deigned to attend to the miseries of his constituents, instead of sinking into the arms of *Thaïs* or *Phryné*, etc." Alceste lives in *Augustodunum*: one day, he travels to Paris, where he lodges with his cousin. He hurries in his desire to take in all the monuments of the capital; near the Palais de Bourbon, he crosses the path of a carriage held immobile by an obstruction of conveyances; and here Archytas appears at the carriage window. Alceste is touched to see *in vita reali* this man who had been but a name and image, and who now gives him an amiable wave of the hand; for Archytas understands that he has been recognized, and he would not be that which he is, if he had ever neglected an elector. Alceste, flattered, returns to the depths of his province, and henceforth vituperates *Aristocles*.

•

Acis no longer shews himself on social media; his friends lament, or gently chide. "How long, Acis, since you changed your profile engraving on the Book of Faces; are you indisposed; or have you become an enemy to mankind?"

"On the contrary: it is only when I absent myself, *Cleon*, that I am reconciled with my fellow man; in that strange land, persons are changed into their contraries as if by a kind of sorcery. I thought *Theobalde* was a Wit, and several times a day he strings together foolish comments; I thought *Polyphemus* a gentleman, and he hoots at great men like a melancholy fishmonger; I thought *Eutyphron* a philosopher, and he hotly disputes every futile topic; I thought *Daphnis* an author, and every phrase he writes on the Book is less than middling; I thought *Menalque* a scholar immersed in study, and he proves exceedingly preoccupied with actresses; I thought *Cydias* humble, and I find him infatuated with his life's every vicissitude; I thought *Pyrame* reasonable, and he shows himself to be a pedant who holds forth upon great events, bedroom rumors, or the weather—in sum, upon every thing—as if the world were at a loss without his learned lessons to know how it should comport itself; I thought *Antisthenes* a wise man, and I see him catch flame at every debate and cry anathema against anyone who holds a different opinion. What unfortunate face, unknown to me thus far, would I reveal if I ventured too long in these precincts?"

•

Damis has written a book, and though he harbors no aversion to success, it pains him to promote himself on the Book of Faces. It is not that he is modest, but rather that he deems it unbecoming of a Wit to serve as town crier of his own praise. He will not say, "Today,

Hégésippe has reviewed my work in *Le Mercure*," but he *will* say, "I am much obliged to Hégésippe for his article in *Le Mercure*, etc."

•

The young Duke of E—— was tall, with pleasant features, and had been educated by the kingdom's finest tutors, who praised his talent for philosophy; he was not unaware of the interest provoked by his person, nor of the attention that hung upon his every word. One day, he found himself ensnared in one of those *mailing lists* that mingle courtiers' names with those of lesser station. Soon, one of the recipients asked to be removed, for an obscure motive which no one can remember; then a second, and a third, etc., all with the same request. They burdened their mailboxes at an ever more rapid pace, by replying each to all. The more they clamored to be removed from the list, the more they inspired in others the self-same wish. Without fully knowing it, they were themselves the cause of this flood of messages against which they railed. The young Duke of E——, who could not but conceive that these many entreaties were addressed to he who held the greatest influence and renown, soon replied to all: "Sirs, I pray you, cease to ask this of me!"

10

AN OLD TRADITION—BUT ONE whose authenticity is highly questionable—holds that in ancient Rome, generals parading in triumph upon their return from a victorious campaign were accompanied on their chariot by a slave whose sole function was to whisper phrases in their ear that exhorted them to modesty, in order to counterbalance the honors and praise that were heaped upon them: remember that you will die, remember that you are only human, etc. One can read in older works of history that this slave was called the *carnifex gloriae*, the butcher of glory; this is most likely a matter of a mistaken interpretation of a passage from Pliny the Elder, but it is so seductive that anyone can easily see why it made such headway. We, too, have our *carnifices gloriae interretiales*. Every individual who attains the least bit of notoriety is sure to see, on the internet, a few not very obliging *comments* attached to his name, scrawled by people who seem to think that the principal justification of their existence is to chastise renown as soon as they see it rear its head.

•

"At the end of my life," wrote Jean Guitton in his memoirs published in 1988, "I can say that I have never stepped into a room in which I was about to speak without experiencing anguish and trembling.

My ideal lecture would be delivered by whispering in the dark. I should have been born at the close of this century, when television has made it possible to speak in private to thousands, with each person at home. It's a miracle that one inner life can communicate, unmediated, through the *media*, with another inner life. Like the invention of the printing press, this electronic world will transform human relations. Writing will give way to the speaking Image: there will no longer be spectators or auditors, but only consciousnesses present to each other."

It isn't surprising that this dream was expressed by a Catholic philosopher. It recalls the utopia of a language of angels which long occupied scholastic theologians; Jean-Louis Chrétien, in an article published by the review *Critique* in 1979, brought to light the poetry of this theme and the timelessness of its implications. Angels are immaterial; this implies, first, that their interiority is not enveloped in an opaque body, and, second, that their thought is not hindered by the mediation of signs. They have never known the difficulty we have in translating our thoughts into words; they recognize no difference between the signifier and the signified. Their consciousnesses communicate with each other lucidly and transparently, without hindrance, without the imperfections encountered in human attempts at expression. They live in immediacy, in the ideal effacement of the sign, in presence to themselves and to others— which hasn't stopped theologians from asking whether angels can keep secrets, and often replying in the affirmative.

The development of the internet has given rise to many discourses whose terms recall those of Guitton's prophecy: according to these claims, exponential advances in mediation paradoxically favor the advent of immediacy; presence, transparency, and therefore truth will win out over distance, misunderstanding, and hypocrisy, faults belonging to an archaic stage of human communication. Guitton imagined—with a fair amount of prescience, in fact—a generalization of televisual communication that resembles what we experience today, but only in part, for there is a whole swath of digital expression that, on the contrary, rests upon anonymity and the secret concealed within the written sign.

Moreover, the written sign doesn't block the progress of a certain form of presence. The dualism that opposes writing to orality as living presence proves, in practice, too crude to correspond to the nuances or paradoxes of reality—and in particular to reality as observed on the internet. The written sign is at once the instrument of a denuding of souls and the only weapon of denuded souls who attack each other mercilessly, with all the violence of civil war. This violence is a test of presence. If these souls showed themselves to each other clothed in their bodies—their faces—and speaking to each other, it is likely that they would recover the restraint, reserve, and distance upon which the possibility of peace is founded.

•

It has often been said that anonymity is a condition of truth telling, for the fundamental anxiety of democratic times is that the tyrant—or an oligarchy—may persecute the individual who speaks the truth without a mask. But masks can also shield or encourage gratuitous absurdities uttered in the hope of not being held to account, or violence that springs from a pure and simple pleasure in doing evil.

We are so used to being on our guard against hypocrisy—and to assuming that kind words are spoken by obligation, for the benefit of society—that we tend to consider spitefulness more authentic, more sincere. The experience of the internet should teach us to cast aside such a prejudice. Though the internet at first confirms our faith in the sincerity of masks, it soon exhausts and reverses this belief.

•

Duns Scotus—as Jean-Louis Chrétien has shown—was one of the Scholastics most hostile to the idea that angels are able to keep secrets. The transparency of the angelic world, for him, admits of no exception. It is the rule and must be absolute. Saint Thomas Aquinas holds that the perfect communication of angels depends upon their will, which orients their thought toward others—without the least seepage between interiority and exteriority—and that their will can also hold back this communication, thereby preventing their thought from reaching others. Duns Scotus says, on the contrary, that not even the very will to conceal—let alone the content—could be hidden from the spiritual vision of angels, who encounter no bodily obstacle when they look at each other. An angel can't hide anything from another angel; an angel can know everything about another angel.

•

In Stalin's time, you got rid of a person by erasing every last trace of him. Today this task is accomplished by exhibiting every last inch of him to public view.

•

One summer day about fifteen years ago, on a wharf in Porquerolles, I very distinctly heard someone say on his mobile phone that he was in the street—and no ambiguity of surroundings or imprecision of expression could reasonably explain the use of the word *street* in reference to this pier. He was a man in the prime of life, accompanied by a woman who looked younger than him.

Mobile phones, which initially made lying easier (with a landline, it was much harder to claim to be at home when in fact you weren't), are about to make lying impossible, now that they know our location at every instant and seem highly eager to communicate it to others, whether to companies or to our "contacts" whom these devices seem inclined to consider universally friendly or well-disposed. They don't generally do this without asking our permission, but it's conceivable they might one day stop worrying about our authorization and start automatically informing our contacts of our whereabouts. If this evolution takes place, it wouldn't be absurd to imagine that telephones will remain more often in offices or homes, at the bottom of a drawer, immobile and well-behaved, and that it will become common not to keep them constantly with us anymore. In this way, they will be reunited with their old ancestor the home phone, like those animal species who returned to the aquatic life their forebears had left behind to conquer the Earth.

•

PSYCHOPATHOLOGY OF DIGITAL LIFE, 9.—From H.: "Six months after the events, when he attempted to analyze them calmly,

Emmanuel Todd spoke of a *totalitarian flash* in describing the collective reactions to the January 2015 Paris attacks. I'm not sure I've understood exactly what he meant by this phrase, and I have a feeling that, if I did, I probably wouldn't agree with what he was trying to say. However, these two words struck me, for they resonated with a fleeting impression that had haunted me during those days, and later as well, but which I was never able to formulate. You know I've been on Facebook for a very long time, but I only post a terse update every six months or so. From time to time, I visit it anyway, to see what's become of my acquaintances or to witness—more or less in spite of myself—what they have on their minds. When the attacks occurred, I spent hours on Facebook following the chain of events and the countless flood of horrified reactions. I was there, watching, but I wrote nothing, shared nothing, posted nothing. I didn't put the *I am Charlie* logo in place of my profile picture, which, for that matter, hasn't changed in years. Then it occurred to me that someone might look at my page, see its relative inactivity, and find fault with me. For the logic of a social network—the outcome toward which its conception and operation tend—is that you share everything you are thinking or feeling at each instant. Not to share is not to feel. Wouldn't I be accused of not having had the right emotion? The mere fact of not having testified to what was taking place in my heart might cast suspicion upon me. All of a sudden I understood that mind control, that old science-fiction fantasy, was an incredibly tangible possibility. But this wasn't thanks to some extravagant machine capable of reading minds, as the Hollywood screenwriters had imagined it; all it had taken to achieve this was that the spontaneous and continuous expression of every last thought had become a social norm. The following week, for the first time, I had a dream composed almost entirely of fictitious Facebook status updates."

•

The internet has written a new chapter in the history of infamy. *Damnatio memoriae*—the punishment of oblivion that the Romans imposed upon some of their emperors, whose statues were toppled and whose names were erased from the public monuments—would naturally be an even harsher penalty in our time, as the space for posterity has been greatly stretched and harbors names that formerly wouldn't have been deemed worthy of even a footnote. But it wouldn't be easy to accomplish. What was deleted from one place would always reappear in another. This way of doing things would be too contrary to the material's inner tendency: the internet abhors a nonentity and hungers for exhibition; exhibition is the element in which the internet burns the victims upon which it feeds each day. The simplest thing to do is to follow this tendency by leaving one's prey a prisoner to the web; for the difficult thing today isn't to become known but rather to be forgotten. Never has Phaedra's cry of anguish—"Where can I hide? For Hades' night I yearn"—resonated with such force; never has it been so common.

•

The phenomenon of digital infamy is like a powerful wave that lifts a person to the height of notoriety, no matter how uncomfortable this elevation might be in rough weather. The individuals who are the most laughed at or hated on the internet are often the ones who give us the most intense sensation of a kind of disturbing electric *aura* when we encounter them by chance in the physical world. Some of them seem to be fully aware of this, and to have wittingly signed this Faustian pact. On a smaller scale than digital infamy, a "social media controversy," whether intentional or not, appears to have become a necessary stage in the creation of any notoriety whatsoever.

•

PSYCHOPATHOLOGY OF DIGITAL LIFE, 10.—Conversation with Z.: "You were somewhat acquainted with W., I think. You know how he is; or rather, you surely remember how he was. A metaphysician through and through; one of our generation's most powerful analysts of the human mind; someone who seemed incapable of yielding to the seduction of the world. He spent ten years deciphering Husserl's manuscripts; he was awarded the bronze medal of the Centre National de la Recherche Scientifique at age thirty-five. Well, believe it or not, I ran into him two weeks ago on the boulevard Saint-Michel and barely recognized him, he looked so haggard and ravaged. When he saw I was about to leave him after a brief exchange of pleasantries, he grabbed my arm with an urgent, almost mad gesture, terribly anxious. I pitied him; I invited him to sit down with me in the little veranda of the Balzar, on rue des Écoles, right next to the boulevard. That's where he told me his story.

"'I wanted to join a social network to see how they function and why people are interested in them,' he said. 'I had every intention of keeping my distance. One day, on a purely experimental basis,

I posted a text on Facebook: very short, fairly witty I think, or in any case above average in its composition. When I saw the first *likes* appear, I felt a pretty strong adrenaline rush. After three hours, I had received about twenty, which I considered an honorable result for someone who had never been active on this network. Several people, having realized that I was now on the network, asked to become friends. I myself sent out a few friend requests to people whom I had lost sight of; these requests were accepted. All of this produced in me an agreeable and fairly novel sensation. A week later, I posted a photo. A photo of my cat walking cautiously over a row of Heidegger books, German editions, on my bookshelf. It was a hit. It was liked fifty-five times, and shared by four or five people. A girl I had been in love with at the lycée wrote a comment saying it was *so cute* and left a winking smiley. I still remember the moment in the midafternoon when I saw the *likes* becoming more and more numerous, as if it would go on forever. I felt my Being, as I rarely had before; I had the impression of pushing back the limits of my individual existence, expanding myself, as it were. It was incredibly intoxicating.'

"At this moment, W. finished his Perrier with a slice of lemon and hailed the waiter to order another; then he went on with his story.

"'I waited three days before posting again. It was a little text, probably not quite as good as the previous one. For a large part of the afternoon, I couldn't tear my eyes away from the little notifications icon. I found the sensation I was looking for, but it wasn't as strong. I got fewer *likes*; I felt a certain resentment. I realized that I had to take things in hand. Several of my friends, who weren't even media stars, would often get between one hundred and one hundred and fifty *likes* for their posts; why shouldn't I be able to do the same?

I launched a second wave of friend requests and began to follow those I already had, as it became clear that if I didn't like their posts, they wouldn't like mine either.'

"W. stopped for an instant, ran his fingers through his disheveled hair.

"'That's when my life took a new course. For days on end, I followed the Facebook news feed, liking and commenting on the posts of others, posting nonstop myself. Each of my posts began with that agonizing and thrilling moment, like a leap into the void: And what if, this time, no one likes it? But no, the little red notifications square would appear, I would receive my first *likes*, then others following one after another with increasing frequency, reaching a peak and then finally ebbing, to signal that my status update's life span had nearly reached its end. I was lifted by a wave of euphoria as if bursts of endorphins were breaking free inside me. But this sensation always seemed too brief; I couldn't wait to experience it again. It became more and more difficult for me to work. At the time, I was supposed to turn in an article for *Revue de métaphysique et de morale*. I never managed to finish it. I haven't written anything at all since that day, except Facebook posts. My great treatise on exo-phenomenology is at a standstill. However, I have written a lot of Facebook posts. Perhaps someday people will realize that my philosophic oeuvre has been here all along, on Facebook.'

"W. took out his phone and set it on the little round table. He was feverish, incapable of keeping his eyes from it. There was a faint *bing* and he pounced on the device.

"'Ah! Two new notifications at once. Some people who like, and someone who's sent me a friend request....Who is this person.... Don't know him....An anonymous admirer, no doubt....I have almost two thousand friends now, you know.... Look, Elsa C. posted an anthology of spelling mistakes she found in her student's papers.... I'll like it.... Sorry, I have to post something now.... I'll take a photo on the sly of the waiter with the big mustache and the white apron. I'll post it with a phrase from *Being and Nothingness*.... I'll get a heap of *likes* with that one....'

"My presence no longer interested him very much. I watched him take the photograph and post it. He worked at incredible speed. The first *likes* appeared at once; his eyes lit up. For an instant, he ceased to be the lost man whose silhouette had startled me on the boulevard Saint-Michel. I pretended to have an appointment and got up to leave; he silently bade me goodbye with a wave of his hand."

•

PSYCHOPATHOLOGY OF DIGITAL LIFE, II.—From L.: "Basically, if I had to sum up my Facebook experience, I'd say it's the continuous revelation of the idiocy of intelligent people. For a long time, I found it hard to believe what I took to be a nasty myth. But the scales have fallen from my eyes. All I have to do is log in, and the horrific certainty forces itself upon me again, with ever more crushing strength. This spectacle fascinates and terrifies me at the same time; I can watch it for hours, silently and invisibly; by the end, I find myself plunged into an emptiness from which I can hardly rise."

•

If there is a deeper causal connection between war and technology than that which explains technological development as an effect of belligerent nations' search for decisive force, and if war in fact results from humanity's malignant and irrepressible desire to use the technological means or potentialities it has at its disposition, then we should fear the extraordinary confrontations that will, so to speak, be summoned by the invention of the internet.

•

Universal exhibition is a conflict of exhibitions. The fear Plato expressed in regard to writing—that texts can fall into the wrong hands, far from their authors, who are unable to defend themselves —finds new confirmation every second on the internet.

•

PSYCHOPATHOLOGY OF DIGITAL LIFE, 12.—L., again: "The irenicism of Facebook's early years is only a memory now, even though neither the functions nor the layout have changed much. We still only have *friends*, and we still only have the option to *like* things. But the continuous outpouring of minds has led me to discover many enemies—among my *friends*."

•

We will become Other, perhaps because we want to (many people dispute this), but above all because we will have become impossible.

•

There are entire swaths of the internet where humanity oddly persists in making sure that its absence would not be regretted and unwittingly offers arguments for its own extinction and transmutation.

•

The internet has brought to light the convergence of the two great Nietzschean ideas, eternal return and the advent of the superhuman. We will more and more often find our path strewn with things that we have done or thought in the past. Are we sufficiently morally armed for this? The absence of forgetfulness is a terrifying weapon in the hands of those all-too-human passions: stupidity, animosity, and resentment.

•

Imagine a scenario, à la WikiLeaks or the Sony Pictures hack, in which someone—either God, or a supercomputer, or the internet itself emerging as a kind of self-aware monster—reveals everyone's data to everyone. It hardly matters whether this results from an accident or a decision. We'll be like those people whose nakedness or sex lives have been projected to the whole world against their will, either by the maliciousness of others or by their own clumsiness —people whom we have pitied or mocked, without adequately conceiving they were the precursors of a new human condition that would one day be our own. We will see each other, all pornographers, all hypocrites, all slanderers of our friends behind their backs, all haunted by unsuspected fantasies and fears, etc. (One of WikiLeaks' principal effects has been to make a mockery of diplomacy, the art of pronouncing friendly words while thinking treacherous ones.) Each person's private life will reveal more than enough reasons to be outraged, offended, grieved, flabbergasted. But what for? The comedy of human morals will be over; we'll no longer be able to pretend to raise ourselves by mocking or blaming others. We won't be able to change a single thing about ourselves. So our morals will change instead.

●

This scenario will be perfected once each of our mental acts leaves an electronic footprint, a piece of "data." This day isn't very far off; even now, the internet's gradual intrusion into the totality of our existence has already reached a stage where the enactment of this hypothetical scenario would completely topple our system of values.

●

Our morals are made for hypocritical societies, where the only thing that counts is what you say, not what you think; what you show to others, not what you secretly are. This isn't a value judgment; it's a historical description. Hypocrisy is a cease-fire in the war of all against all that silently rages in each of our hearts. The obliteration of the boundary between private and public life will force us to find other ways of keeping the peace. The internet will teach us to be more likable, or less touchy. We aren't mature enough for this invention.

11

OUR COMPUTERS AND TELEPHONE SCREENS are linked to every ramification of our existence, from our sensations and passions, to the castles we build in the air and our most trivial actions, and they hold an ever greater share in the emotional memory that links us to our past, not only because of the infinite archives to which they give access but also because they grow old with us and acquire in turn a flavor of old-fashioned things. They live at the heart of perceptory experiences and thought processes that hold inexhaustible riches, if only we take the trouble to deploy them in literature; they are no less worthy as a literary subject than a candle flame, the color of autumn leaves, the millstone walls of the Valois, the paving stones of courtyards behind carriage gateways, the scents of Arabia, or our visits with our old aunts on Sundays for tea.

•

As I was writing this book, my computer broke down. One of its sides had been in contact with some water, which must have seeped inside. I thought the computer was lost and several weeks of work along with it. Foolishly, I had put off making a backup. I was working on three or four projects, which were advancing slowly. I kept saying to myself: Wait, wait just a little longer, another page, another two pages, and then, only then, you'll back all of this up externally. I was courting disaster, in the guise of forcing myself to make progress. I hadn't been worried enough about losing these files that were far from finished and didn't satisfy me; when it happened, I thought the ground had given way beneath my feet. From this book, not without a certain irony, about twenty pages disappeared in which I had held forth on the impossibility of ever losing anything anymore, or rather—and I felt that I had learned, at my own cost, to remember this nuance—on the dream of such an impossibility.

I was supposed to leave for Brittany; I didn't reschedule my trip. Perhaps it would help me to forget this incident that was starting to eat away at me. Aside from A., who was coming along with me, I hadn't had time to speak of it to anyone, or to take my computer to a tech specialist, which I planned to do as soon as I got back. Less than forty-eight hours had passed since the accident when we left. The computer hadn't started up again; drying out in the meantime hadn't done it any good; I had hoped it might. I spent the days of this vacation stricken with uncertainty, wavering between the misgiving that I would have to start from scratch with all the work that hadn't been backed up, and the hope that it might be possible to recover it, even if that meant losing the machine—a hope that a few internet forums I had consulted right before my departure seemed to support. The second hypothesis helped me to bear the first. The serenity with which I stoically prepared to accept the irretrievable loss of this data rested largely upon the possibility that in reality the data hadn't been lost at all, a ruse I was well aware of.

I had heard several of my friends tell me how they had lost articles or even entire books that had been only on their computers; I had admired their apparent nonchalance, while imagining the supreme despair into which I would have fallen if the same thing had happened to me. Of course, I'd had a few mishaps, but they hadn't greatly affected me. In 2007—I believe it was 2007—on rue de Turenne I let slip from my pocket a USB flash drive that held the only copy of two pages I had just written of a novel that had been in progress for several years. Once lost, these pages seemed to be the most beautiful pages I had ever written. I never tried to rewrite them. I undoubtedly would have, someday, if that novel had ever come to anything. The loss crushed my inspiration, although it already had, and would continue to have, other reasons to falter. *Ocean Kingdom*—that was the title—wasn't a good text. I only admitted this to myself later, but I probably already had an inkling of it when I was, or feigned to be, thwarted in my momentum by the disappearance of these pages. That didn't happen right away, however, and I blush to think that my principal fear at the time, as I distinctly remember, was that a passerby might find my USB stick and publish the opening of my brilliant novel in his own name. At the moment, the principal profit this incident yielded was the moral lesson I drew from it and still maintain, even if, out of weakness, I sometimes fail to hold by it. When I have doubts about a work in progress, when I think I can't go on and am considering giving up, I tell myself that if I were to lose the work in some digital accident, I would find it magnificent in retrospect and start weeping my eyes out.

The aura of things glimpsed once and then lost forever is so great that at times it still occurs to me that the mislaid pages of *Ocean Kingdom* might not have been the worst of the book. They were at the beginning of part 2. At the end of part 1, two friends had entered the Port of Barcelona on a sailboat, in the first light of morning, after a difficult night in which they had been caught in a gale. There was the narrator—the one who said "I," my alter ego—and there was the crewmate. They had moored the boat and fallen asleep. The lost pages described their waking, at noon—"When I woke, it was noon" (I remember just now having given in to the temptation of inserting this hidden quotation from Rimbaud, which confirms my suspicion that this text was rife with flaws). The sun's rays, passing through the hatchway, had half awoken the narrator; in his drowsiness, he could hear children's voices and the footsteps of people walking along the wharf; through a half-closed eye, he saw a line of golden light glimmer on a swath of varnished wood. He rose; outside, in the cockpit, he found his crewmate already up, with a vaguely victorious air at having spent less time sunk in sleep. Then, while drinking a coffee, he described to his crewmate a dream he had just had—and which I truly had, me, M.R., but in Paris and not on a boat.

He was on a beach and had just stepped out of the water. The light was a deep, incandescent yellow; it came from nowhere; it seemed to emanate from objects, from things themselves; it was like a beautiful sunset with no sun. I had written one or two sentences heavily inspired by a passage that had struck me in Nerval's *Aurélia*, for it profoundly resonated with the memory of this dream, the memory of its strange illumination: "It is a well-known fact that no one ever sees the sun in a dream, although one is often aware of some far brighter light. Material objects and human bodies are illumined through their own agencies." As he walked toward the sand, the narrator saw bodies of women and men being born inside the waves that broke upon the shore, bodies as vaporish and white as the sea foam, but slightly gilded, too. He was surprised; on the beach he found his father, whom he questioned about this disturbing phenomenon. His father, who, like mine, always had an answer to every

question a child can ask, now explained to him, as naturally as can
be, that it was well known that on this shore the departed beings
you thought about were reconstituted by the sea. This dream, when
I myself had it, was obviously inspired by Tarkovsky's *Solaris*, which
I must have rewatched not long before.

At the time, I thought these vanished pages were so perfect that
I felt incapable of rewriting them. Eventually, I came to associate
them with another phenomenon in which dreams also played a role.
On several occasions, I have dreamt of imaginary books whose perfect sentences captivated me in my sleep but then completely vanished from my memory upon waking. In 2003 or 2004, over an
interval of a few months, I dreamt of an imaginary novel by Gilles
Deleuze and of another by Bernard Pautrat, who had been my adviser
in the philosophy department at the École Normale Supérieure.
Pautrat had once shown me a work from Deleuze's youth—it's no
coincidence, then, that they were both involved, not exactly together
but in the same way, in these dreams. It was a bizarre and impossible-
to-find text, disavowed, buried by Deleuze in the deepest oblivion,
a preface to an esoteric book published in the 1940s, perhaps during
the Occupation (I have forgotten the exact date) but in any case
written when Deleuze was still a very young man of almost diabolical
intelligence, a student at the university or perhaps even at the lycée,
where his brilliance already attracted a following. This text of
Deleuze's, as I am describing it, sounds itself like something imaginary; but, I beg my reader to believe me, it really exists.

In these dreams, I would read only a few opening pages of these
invented novels, the opening ones; they were enough to excite me,
to make me feel as if the mystery of absolute writing—which I probably would have defined then as the conjunction of pure music and

high philosophy—had been resolved and even revealed to me by the visitations of sleep. Others appeared as the authors of these texts; but the dreams, after all, were mine, and I appropriated the texts without much scruple. Sometimes, in the midst of a dream, I acquire a kind of uncertain awareness of my state, and this second self soon came to lie in wait for such treasures. But as the moment of waking approached, I would have a presentiment of how difficult it would be to retain, in conscious life, the memory of all these glimpsed magical pages. I was like a prospector who finds heaps of gold coins or nuggets in a remote hiding place and, drunk at first with joy and then with rage, realizes that his pockets will only hold a minuscule portion of it. I clung to the conviction that a few sentences would suffice to initiate me into in the secrets of absolute writing; even a single phrase, if I kept hold of it, would serve as a viaticum to extend my mental powers, would make my mind a fountainhead from which, infinitely and effortlessly, rivers of magnificent phrases would spring. At last I would begin to emerge from sleep, my eyes still shut; the transition from the dream's second self to this embryonic waking state had been relatively imperceptible. This was the moment of truth; I struggled to grab words, but they all fled faster and faster, as through the neck of an hourglass. When I opened my eyes, the sublime pages were utterly gone; I didn't have the slightest idea of what they had said.

Back when I was writing speeches for François Fillon at Matignon, I twice saw Word files that I had just finished, and that I absolutely had to turn in that very day, disappear before my eyes. I was distraught, but I didn't have time to yield to despair. I had to rewrite the text at all costs. I had about three hours ahead of me. I was all nerves, pressure, extreme memory. Line by line, I found the phrases at my fingertips. They weren't lost; and, as painful as the experience was, I came out of it with an unexpected, fierce satisfaction.

This fierce satisfaction called to mind yet another episode. At the very beginning of the 2000s, I had begun a translation of Paul Celan's "Death Fugue." I hadn't finished it. The handful of lines I had translated were written down on a piece of paper buried in one file or another. In 2008, I translated the poem in its entirety for a review, without having tried to find this earlier draft. A little later, it resurfaced as I was filing papers. It was difficult to believe: years apart, my choices had been exactly the same. From this I concluded that we can always hope that what has once been thought is never entirely lost, even if its inscription is misplaced.

The few days I spent in Brittany were mostly devoted to dredging up certain phrases from the lost files, then retaining them, turning them around in mind, attempting to use them as fixed points that might allow other phrases to rise to the surface as well. Behind the wheel of the car, on the deck chairs of the hotel terrace, throughout the long walks we took by the sea, I took every opportunity that arose to steal moments of silence, sometimes very brief, sometimes longer, in which I abandoned myself to this mental deep-sea diving. In the evening, I wrote down the resurrected phrases I had revolved in my mind over the course of the day. How long would it take me to reconstitute my texts as a whole? Would it even be possible? I saw myself entering a period of great asceticism, absolute concentration. The incident might be salutary. I might at last find the strength to cast aside the bad habits of laziness and procrastination that I blamed for making me write too slowly, too little.

I also told myself that the phrases that never came back would be the least accomplished ones, that these repeated dives into my memory would work like the breaking waves polishing pebbles along the shore. Until a fairly advanced age, I naively believed that all writers know every word of their books by heart, that they have their entire oeuvre in their heads. If any authors have ever accomplished such a wonder, they must be rare. It's difficult to accept this evident fact, probably because the image of blind Homer inhabited by his long poems continues to make an impression. But perhaps I now had to convert this belief into an ideal and strive toward the total mental possession of a text, as if this were the sign—as well as the cause—of its purity. If I reached this state, I told myself, I would come out improved from the hardship that had been imposed upon me.

That cursed spring undoubtedly was to be a time of penance. During the same period, some friends had grievances against me. People called me less. In a port in Brittany, my phone rang; it was an unknown number. I had a fleeting sensation that someone, somewhere, had learned of my misfortune and was about to tell me that he had recovered my files. But the phone only rang a few times, and no one left a message; the person on the other end of the line must have realized they had the wrong number.

When we got back to Paris, I went to my computer. I turned it on; it started up. After five days, it must have completely dried out. I compared the passages that I had begun to rewrite in Brittany to the recovered files; the sentences were identical, give or take a word.

•

On several occasions, over the course of the past fifteen years, melodies which seemed almost as perfect as the pages of books read in dream have flashed through my mind. But I have never transcribed them, because I didn't think I would be able to and because—weak desire being as effective a cause of inaction as real incapacity—I told myself that, yes, someday I would revive my old notions of musical notation to collect the new melodies that came my way and perhaps even recover those I had let pass. These little inner epiphanies didn't come frequently enough to force me to carry out this project. In all, this must have happened to me fewer than a dozen times. I probably should have tried to knock together a personal system of notation, to keep a minimal trace of these musical visitations, but this, too, seemed impossible and futile at the time. Sometimes it was chamber music, sometimes club music; I felt as though these melodies were entirely new, but perhaps they were only the recollections of things I had already heard and didn't recognize. I wonder if they will some-day reappear at the surface of my consciousness. My experience with the two texts I had written in identical fashion, years apart from each other, had led me to believe that what has once been thought is never utterly lost, even when it no longer possesses a material inscription. Sometimes I lose all hope in this, sometimes I find it again—I picture myself, then, as a computer in whose depths a skilled technician can recover the files we thought were destroyed.

•

A few weeks after my computer's miraculously resolved breakdown, my smartphone slipped out of my inner jacket pocket and fell into the waters of the port of Le Havre; I had come back and bent down to retie one of the hawsers fastening the boat to the pier. Having already made up my mind to leave, I had taken off my oilskin, whose sealed pockets had perfectly sheltered my phone during even the most acrobatic maneuvers while sailing. I'd had this phone for two and a half years; I lost many photographs and a few videos. I was upset, but my sorrow was nothing like what I would have felt if I had lost a text that had taken several months, weeks, or even days to write. That's how it is; I would speak otherwise if images were my work material. I forced myself not to think about it, not to list everything that had sunk: that's all it would have taken for my absent grief to claim its due.

There was one photograph, however, that I immediately regretted losing. I had taken it the day after the death of my father, a year and a half earlier, in that same city of Le Havre where I had just watched it sink with the others. It was on a winter morning before sunrise; the color of the sky was passing from jet-black to very dark gray. A. and I had stayed in a hotel along the beach, near Sainte-Adresse. In the room, a large bay window overlooked the open sea. I had woken up first. It was the hour at which people were starting to head to work; traffic was heavy on the waterfront boulevard. The city lights were still on and the car headlights radiated through the humid air. The Cathedral of Saint Joseph, like a stark concrete rocket, towered above the scene.

But I could only see the reflection of all this—in nothing short of cinematic dimensions—a reflection that projected itself in the large bay window onto the sea and night sky, as if an entire city had established itself upon the waters; a futuristic city where, indifferent to the mystery or technological feat of its establishment upon the waters, people drove to work each morning and life pursued its course; or else a ghost city, a lost City of Ys whose specter hovered atop the ocean that had engulfed it, reappearing at certain times, moments as ephemeral as this miraculous reflection. The first tendency of this daydream—and, in a way, the second as well, considering that the original city had been almost entirely destroyed—resonated with the modernism of Le Havre as it had been rebuilt by Auguste Perret after the war: the reflection prolonged the city's modernism, accentuated it, carried it across a threshold of poetic transfiguration. In projecting itself onto the ocean, the city also projected itself onto another space and another time, onto another planet, another physics, another technology.

It was the kind of image I associate with the monologue of the humanoid who, at the end of *Blade Runner*, prepares for death by recalling the incredible sights he has seen in distant galactic lands: "I've seen things you people wouldn't believe.... Attack ships on fire off the shoulder of Orion.... I watched c-beams glitter in the dark near the Tannhaüser Gate...." It so happens that a little more than a year before his death, my father had told me that he had recently rewatched *Blade Runner* and that he had greatly enjoyed it, as in years past, or perhaps even more, and in particular this ending. At roughly the same time, without our having planned it, I had also gone back to the film, almost twenty years after last seeing it. My father must have had the feeling, more than he had let on, that he would soon die, and this whole scene, with its simple and sublime conclusion, "time to die," offers a peaceful image of death—unexpectedly so, for the one who speaks these words has led the revolt of the replicants demanding a longer life span from their human creator. In extremis, the feeling of having seen enough beauty and novelty during one's life wins out over the regret at parting from it. I thought my father must have said to himself, "I've seen things," as he remembered his sea journeys; for in remembering those on which I had accompanied him, I said to myself with gratitude, "I've seen things," I've seen things that in those days the classmates with whom I met up again on Monday mornings at school couldn't imagine, I've seen islands of gold enveloped in mist, I've seen columns of sea foam spouting forth beneath our bow in the Teignouse strait, I've seen rosaries of Russian freighters lit up like luxury trains, at night, off the port of Saint-Nazaire.

In fact, nothing in real life so directly evokes for me the opening scene of *Blade Runner* as arriving at Le Havre at night, when you find yourself skirting the industrial zone after having cleared the Tancarville Bridge and you see, dancing against the dark sky, the fire flakes escaping from the refinery's flare stack.

I don't know if the extraordinary play of reflections I saw at the window of that hotel naturally recurs each day. As the light increased, the ocean city faded little by little. I wonder why I didn't film this scene; I know why, I was crushed by my father's death, a thousand things awaited me that somber day, I soon had to leave to meet my mother; the feeling that this wasn't the right time paralyzed me. Even so, I took a photograph which at that moment seemed poor indeed, compared to the spectacle I had before my eyes. Today, I would give a lot to have it again.

•

This story raises other images to the surface of my memory: some photographs I took on a beach in Nice, the day before my abrupt return to Le Havre. It was at the end of the afternoon near a dock that seemed to be a vestige of the old pleasure pier; night was falling, the seafront was lit up, the Baie des Anges was smooth, scintillating like an immense silver mirror, a final expanse of light as earth and sky tilted into shadow. The dark silhouette of a pensive ambler stood motionless on the threshold of this white sea, which traced his form with supernatural sharpness, at the moment when the night was beginning to efface the contours of all things. Lingering a little higher at the edge of the parapet, I stared a long while at this allegory, as I tried to compose a frame in which to carry away its memory.

•

Among the lost photographs of which the memory immediately resurfaced, there were also those I had taken in a little chapel on the northeast end of Cap Corse, on the trail that skirts the shore. From the outside, if I remember correctly, it looked particularly rustic, but inside, the walls were of a cerulean blue that I found exhilaratingly beautiful and of which I took many snapshots. The reason I was upset by their loss was that I had the impression of having captured something rare, unknown, of which I could never recover the trace, except by visiting the place again.

I had even forgotten the name of this chapel. A little later, I went on Google Maps, thinking I might find it there. I zoomed in on the coastal footpath and the name indeed appeared: Santa Maria. But that wasn't all; by clicking on the site of the chapel, you could call up photographs various travelers had taken of it. A few of them reminded me of the ones I had lost. You could see in them the cerulean blue of which I had believed I was the only admirer and witness.

•

Some time ago, A. returned from a voyage to China and told me of a conversation she had overheard between her neighbors on the plane. One man was saying to another sitting at his right, who seemed to be his boss or a superior of a kind, that some old photographs had reappeared on his mobile phone, photographs he barely remembered, taken long before he had acquired his present phone, and probably many earlier phones as well. It was as if the machine had tracked him down and faithfully reconstituted the disjointed elements of his identity. Perhaps the resurrection of images had begun. All I had to do was wait, and I too would see the photographs I thought were gone forever rising to the surface.

•

Which is worse? We are caught in a dilemma between the anxiety of losing everything, irretrievably, without any possible remedy, and that of being read, spied upon, now or later, by a distant stranger. Of the two evils, I confess, the first terrifies me more than the second.

•

The number of questions that the internet is incapable of answering has constantly diminished over the course of the past few years, at an astonishing rate and in significant proportion. When I come upon one of these intractable questions, scarcer and scarcer these days, I get an urge to write it down in a notebook amid a list of other remarkable facts.

For example, when I returned from a holiday at the end of August

2014, I found a postcard from Japan in my mailbox. The signature was difficult to decipher, but it didn't seem incompatible with the name of a friend who, it so happened, had been there that summer. I sent her an email to thank her; she replied that she wasn't the author of the card. I reread it; I really couldn't see who might have sent it. We are less and less familiar with each other's handwriting. Whoever could have sent me a postcard from Japan in July? The simple fact that the internet was of no use in answering this question provoked in me an imperceptible sense of powerlessness that seemed strangely new to me—for in the past, we weren't usually surprised at the impossibility of answering a question.

•

We've become so accustomed to finding everything again, to think-ing we'll always be able to see on the internet whatever we once have seen on it, and to believing that digital extension is the locus of salvation and eternity for all things, that we're surprised and disap-pointed when we can't get hold of pages that have disappeared, as if nature had reasserted her rights over pure spirit and reestablished her reign of generation and decay in this unconquered territory.

•

There is a form of forgetting that is born of excess memory, a form of vanishing that results from an infinite accumulation of data, which we particularly experience when we try—in vain, more often than not—to find a Facebook status or a share that caught our atten-tion a few weeks earlier and has since been engulfed a thousandfold beneath the mass of new messages that have followed one another at every instant on the home page.

•

D., feverish, still moved at having discovered that machines know him better than he knows himself, relates to me the following incident which has just taken place: "I had forgotten whether I had G.'s book or not; I went looking for it on my bookshelves, which, as you know, are many and not always well organized; I didn't find it on the shelves where I thought it might be; I concluded that I didn't have it; I got ready to buy it on Amazon; Amazon told me: *You purchased this item on February 23, 2009.* That was more than five years ago. I had absolutely no memory of it. How far off is the day when my computer can also tell me in what obscure nook of my house I put it down?"

•

PSYCHOPATHOLOGY OF DIGITAL LIFE, 13.—From M.: "When I was on the threshold of adulthood, I could only envision with a certain anxiety the cold labyrinth strewn with Kafkaesque traps that seemed to await me. Faced with a thousand proceedings that I found impenetrable, people everywhere seemed to possess an unlimited knowledge whose sources were hidden from me; it wasn't something you learned in school. My fear of never acquiring it was all the greater in that I could see a moment quickly approaching when I would be ashamed to ask about things that appeared obvious to everyone. Even my own parents would undoubtedly look at me with eyes wide open, having assumed that if I hadn't asked them yet, I must have already been informed of such things through other channels. (I believed I had already experienced this on one occasion.) Scorn and disgrace would descend upon me; society, ever eager to cast into darkness those who neglect its procedures, would find in me an ideal victim; they would inform me that, anyway, it was too late, my case was hopeless, for these were all things I should have learned ages ago.

"The internet sprang into my life at the precise moment when I was about to come face-to-face with these Kafkaesque questions. More often than not, it has the answer; when it doesn't, it gives enough information to put on a decent show of not having neglected the problem at hand, a conscientious attitude much appreciated by representatives of bureaucracy. It was as if the Red Sea had parted before me. This fortunate conjunction between the course of the world and that of my own life never ceases to astonish me when I think of it. I sometimes wonder if, in the past, other individuals have likewise felt that they were saved from an existential predicament by the miraculous advent of a new technology. I've been trying to piece together other comparable situations; so far, I haven't found any."

•

One Saturday afternoon in December 2014, I saw a small map of central Paris spontaneously form at the bottom right of my screen and set itself down on the Word file I was proofreading. I hadn't issued any particular command to summon it, nor—I am certain—had I made any accidental gesture that could have had this result.

Its apparition wasn't completely instantaneous, like that of certain pop-up advertising windows; there was, before the image settled, a slight *duration*, a kind of gradual superposition, strangely cottony, in reality quite brief, but which my memory has come to lengthen by returning to it almost obsessively. It resembled Google Maps but—I am certain of this as well—it was not Google Maps. Two points appeared; one marked my home, where I happened to be at that moment, and the other marked a library in the Latin Quarter I often went to—and next to this point was written: "work." The line of a suggested route traced itself out, with the specification that it would take me exactly seventeen minutes only to get up from my comfortable armchair and arrive at this place where duty called. The thought of going there had just crossed my mind, even though the impending night and bitter cold had already sapped my will. These seventeen minutes corresponded precisely to the time it usually took me to get there, several times a week, by bicycle—a little more than a quarter of an hour, a little less than twenty minutes, I would say to myself. I regret that I was so disconcerted that I retained only a very vague memory of the suggested itinerary; in all likelihood it was none other than the route I indeed would take, by way of rue Saint-Jacques, which was the most rational one anyway, so it's difficult to imagine the machine indicating any other. At no time had I in any way revealed the slightest scrap of this information to my computer, needless to say. I was a little frightened; I hastily closed this small map that knew so much about me, without concerning myself about where it came from or how to call it up again. I thought it would return to visit me without any action on my part. It hasn't reappeared, so far. I watch for it, I lie in wait for it; but I don't yet know if I will rebel against its inquisition and its commandments, or if it will schedule me an outrageous appointment to which I will report like a sleepwalker, in the—trite and mad—hope of starting a new life.

•

The little map returned, at last, three months after its first apparition. I was in the very library that it had previously been so kind as to indicate as my workplace and suggest that it might be time for me to report there. I brushed my touch screen with an involuntary gesture, clumsy and abrupt, in the blank margins of my Word file— which means I *clicked on nothing*—and the map appeared at my fingertip. It showed me the return journey—sixteen minutes, a smaller number—and the place where I live, next to which was written: "home." The library was about to close; the map's intervention was therefore fairly opportune. But I was a little disappointed in it, this time. In the end, it seems to believe that I travel by car, and the route it proposed wasn't the one I usually took home, when I cut through passageways inaccessible to cars. I closed the map; and I immediately tried to make it reappear by rubbing in the margin approximately in the same place but without managing to reproduce the bizarre gesture that had escaped me. This did nothing, of course.

•

At the very beginning of the 2000s, I was trying to gather material on Moulay Ismaïl, sultan of Morocco; I had an idea for a short story in which he would be the main character. I specifically remember— all the more specifically, since I barely used the internet back then, except to write fairly rare emails—that I searched on Google and found nothing, absolutely nothing. The internet had appeared in the mid-1990s; it was born again in the mid-2000s. That's when, judging by my own experience, its function as an infinite archive was added to its function as a network. YouTube was created in 2005, and Google Earth as well. I think it was around this same time that Wikipedia entries became sufficiently numerous and reliable to be consulted about everything and, better yet, to form a labyrinth where you could pleasurably wander from link to link. This is also about the same time that Facebook was developed and launched. These sites represent, as it were, the quintessence of the internet in its current state; for how much longer, no one can tell.

When I began to take these notes in early 2009, I spoke of the internet as if it were a timeless thing, sprung fully armed from Jupiter's head and committed to indefinitely retaining the form in which it had entered into and changed our experience; as if there were a before and an after—a phenomenon that could in itself absorb all our attention—and as if on each side of the dividing line there extended a largely unchanging landscape. Observing over the course of the years that this new landscape was in fact changing, and presuming that it would change further still, in proportions difficult to measure exactly, I acquired the habit of noting the dates of these narratives, so that I might testify to the historicity of these mutations which we have seen and which others will someday in turn relegate to the past. I did this to keep a trace of the thousand constant changes of which this great change will itself have been made.

•

I gave a start and thought, once again, that my computer must indeed know a great deal about me when, as I began to write "proust" in the Google search bar, I saw the machine insistently suggest "proust sailing," as if it had decided to associate—for my convenience, and with a touching and almost clumsy goodwill—the two subjects that have most occupied my life, even though in my mind they couldn't be more distinct from each other. I played along; I came upon the website of a ship chandler that bears this name, established in La Rochelle in 1977. I was disappointed; I was reassured. A little later, I was seized by a slight misgiving; due to the machine's intrusive affection, I perhaps ran the risk of being locked unawares into the narrow world of my "preferences." One day when I found myself in a library that placed at the disposal of its visitors a number of public, neutral computers, I decided to be sure. I took a seat at one of them, I slowly typed "P R O U S" and before I even got to "T," I saw the surprising suggestion "proust sailing" appear once again, at the top of the list, above "proust gaspard." "Proust marcel" only appeared third, followed by "proust quiz." That ship chandler's computer specialist must be a master of search engine optimization.

•

For a few months now, autocomplete features have multiplied at my fingertips. My email constantly wants to correct, behind my back, the names of my interlocutors it doesn't recognize, at the risk of creating comical diplomatic incidents (to resolve them, we ought to plead *lapsus computatri*)—much as Françoise, in Proust, speaks of the Guermantes' "cousin from Algiers," since she has never heard of *Angers*, but knows of *Algiers* "because of some particularly unpleasant dates that used to be given us at the New Year," and she can't rationally conceive that a language could contain two distinct terms whose pronunciation is so similar.

My tablet's Word program is more perceptive, and often proposes exactly the word I want to use. I'm not speaking of prepositions that obviously have to come after a given verb, nor of the all-purpose words that make up the backbone of our sentences, but of far more subtle situations, truly idiosyncratic choices that verge upon stylistic expression. The program has, for example, several times suggested the adverb "singularly," having evidently understood that I occasionally resort to this word to avoid "especially," which inspires in me an instinctive repugnance. This isn't so surprising. It remembers all the texts I have written in the past fifteen years; it has had ample occasion to form a vague idea of my predilections. Far be it from me to take offense at this; I wouldn't mind if, from time to time, the machine would relieve me a little of the infinite labor of placing one word after another. Paul Valéry said that the first line of a poem is given freely by the gods, and then the duty falls to us to fashion others not unworthy of their "supernatural eldest sibling." It's your turn, machine, to form phrases worthy of the first lines we offer you.

•

Our deepest desire—or the one I find in myself, at any rate—is probably not to possess a machine that would think in our stead but rather to become ourselves a machine whose thoughts we can admire without effort.

•

We know that, among the ancient Greeks, mental activities were held to be the prerogative of free persons and were considered not work but leisure, and that the sphere of manual labor—or of material life in general—was the province of slaves, or at least of persons considered inferior. Aristotle's ironic dream, which says that if tools could execute or even anticipate commands on their own then there would no longer be any need for slaves, is limited to this sphere.

In reality, mental activities are also work, productive efforts that have their share of monotony and repetition, processes of voluntary servitude. To write, we have to become slaves to an idea or a form. Otherwise, nothing gets expressed, nothing rises from its initial nebulous state. Therefore, it isn't surprising that we dream of machines for this too, and are closer and closer to having them.

•

Aristotle also holds that the ultimate stage of self-mastery—intellectual and moral—would be as perfectly regulated as the circular, uniform, and eternal movement of stars in the superlunary world.

•

In a sci-fi film, a police officer says to an individual he has just unmasked as a humanoid robot: "You can't write a novel or a concerto." The robot replies: "Can you?"

Our wariness at the prospect of artificial intelligence possibly rests upon an even greater fear than that of being annihilated, enslaved, replaced, etc. by machines (though we are quick to portray this as an irreparable loss to the universe): the fear of being unmasked as feeble, humdrum creatures, mostly incapable of creating anything at all.

We spend our time uttering phrases that have already been uttered. We constantly copy and paste each other. People have always thought the distinction between a robot and a human showed itself in the differences between their replies, in their mental creations. This difference is lessening at a dizzying rate, not only through the perfecting of machines but also through our increasing capacities for reduplication, which bring our operations closer in line with theirs. To a greater and greater extent, we are content to draw raw components from a gigantic stock of information, only to reproduce these components more or less as we found them, through mimicry, idleness, or lack of skill. Instead of endlessly interrogating our poor computers, we should rather ask ourselves whether the millions of interchangeable documents produced each week by marketing departments, universities, administrations, political orators, etc., all over the world, wouldn't in the eyes of an impartial observer—or even in our own eyes if we managed to shed our pride—appear to be an honest accumulation of symbols automatically generated by machines endowed with a fairly meager share of wit. The distinction between human and machine no longer rests upon external phe-nomena but rather upon inner process, and this last refuge will undoubtedly be conquered in turn.

The machine is not external to us. We are machines more often than we are non-machines; we are non-machines only insofar as we are neurotic or creative. But we have to be machines; we have to be machines to follow through with a task, to give body to the fleeting vision of an idea, etc. We don't have to rebel proudly against our becoming-machine, which has always existed; rather, we need to rid ourselves of the blindness that pushes us to seek, at all costs, to differentiate ourselves from machines, at the very moment when our machine part is seeing such considerable growth in its faculties.

•

We are automatons as much as we are minds, said Pascal. It's becoming more and more evident that we are automatons *insomuch as* we are minds.

•

In *Logics of Worlds*, Alain Badiou writes that an *event* is a "real change [...] that absolutizes the inexistent": something that existed as little as possible—something that was, as we say, "there but not there"— suddenly attains a maximal degree of existence, at the end of a process of greater or lesser abruptness, greater or lesser silence, depending upon the circumstances. In this total upheaval of the configuration of things, an old world dies, a new world appears.

When I was a child, in the 1980s, we had computers at home fairly early, probably a little sooner than average, and their punctual upgrades kept brisk pace with the advances in computing. My father, who was a civil servant in the French Postes, Télégraphes et Téléphones agency at the time, would also bring us the latest Minitel models as soon as they came out. And he had laptop computers, which must have been very rare, and very expensive, since he let me know that I shouldn't hope to play for even a single second with these machines, whereas he usually treated such requests with indulgence and generosity.

I remember being intrigued by the @ key—which I found very pretty and which we never used—on the keyboard of one of our first computers. Its strangely ornamental graphics clashed with the austerity of the other keys—numbers, letters, and punctuation marks that reminded me of the schoolrooms where we learned how to use them. Here was a key that had nothing to do with the crudely abstract images produced by computers at the time, primitive machines that seemed radically incapable of ever representing the inexhaustible richness of the physical world, reserved only for cinema and television. I think this even led me to ascribe certain magical powers to the key. If ever a pumpkin was to turn into a coach—or if ever a monochrome block unfit for reproducing the slightest formal beauty or chromatic variety was to transcend the narrow limits of its current condition—I was sure this enigmatic key would have a part in the miracle. Perhaps the computer had hidden within itself the secret to its own transmutation; in that case, the @ key was a discreet sign of this, a clue. I didn't even know its name; I probably called it "the snail."

I remember finally asking my father. I had to make him repeat his answer several times: "*arobase*"—which redoubled the enigma instead of solving it. I had hoped the name would harbor the meaning, at least in part; that wasn't the case. On the other hand, I have no recollection at all of the explanations he gave, or tried to give, about the key's function. I'm only certain that they were brief and that I remained unsatisfied.

When I try to reconstruct his answer, two possibilities come to mind, which might both be true. He must have known this key had long existed on typewriter keyboards (his father sold Olivetti type-writers in Saint-Brieuc), but was he aware (as we can easily learn today on the internet) that this was because nineteenth-century American shopkeepers had used it to designate merchandise unit prices on accounting forms (10 eggs @ $1)? The other possibility is that he told me the @ was used only for functions that far exceeded the capacities of our humble machines, and were too prosaic to interest a child anyway. The current form of email addresses, with its central @, had been invented at the very beginning of the 1970s. I can no longer ask my father exactly what he knew about the internet at the moment I have in mind, which was in the mid-1980s. It's hard to believe he was completely in the dark about it; he must have heard of it, without being privy to the details. Retrospectively, people have reproached the French elite for having been besotted with the spirit of abstraction that gave rise to the Minitel, and not having paid enough attention to the potential developments of the internet, whose empirical, or even makeshift, aspect inspired in them a hint of disdain. I know my father didn't share this blind self-satisfaction, and he often lamented, skeptically and ironically, the inertia of the system in which he worked; but I can't positively state that he foresaw better than anyone else what was about to happen. In any case, I was disappointed to learn that the @ key was useless and held no mystery. It lost its charm and I stopped noticing it. Did I try to ask other people, my classmates, my secondary-school science teachers? I can't remember; I don't think so. If I did, no one managed to give me a better answer.

A few years later, I saw the @ key reappear in all its majesty. Everyone used it constantly for email addresses. It had become the emblem of the internet; it was glamorous, irresistible. We notice it less now that it has become one of the most familiar and obvious elements of our existence, like any letter of the alphabet or punctuation mark—and it is in fact a hybrid of these two semantic species, which seem to have cohabited for so long that they finally had a child together. Its useless presence on keyboards for so many years clearly had incidental causes. But who could resist slipping into the dream of a strange premonition, as if it were written somewhere that the world would one day be conquered by a fifth column composed of all the copies of this frivolous, vain, overlooked, or pitied key, whose destiny no one suspected.

•

I must have learned of the existence of the internet in 1996—but it could have been late 1995 or early 1997—from a long article in *Le Monde* announcing that this invention was about to change our lives. I admit I wasn't particularly moved; at the time, I was about to enter a period of total asceticism that would last two years, during which I absorbed myself in the study of the past, cutting myself off from the contemporary world with a radicality that impresses me even now and an abnegation of which I would be incapable today.

When I matriculated at the École Normale Supérieure in September 1998, one of the first things we received was an email address, with a randomly generated password. The email account has long since been closed, but I still use the password from time to time— I've just altered it slightly over the years. In one of the rooms of the library, we were invited to a "training session" that consisted in sitting us down at a computer and showing us how to use a search engine—it must have been AltaVista. I blush to think with what detached boredom I heeded this brief session; but I don't think I was any less attentive than my classmates and, in our defense, the act of typing "keywords" into a box already seemed such an intuitive and natural exercise that it was perhaps not absurd to regard with slight derision the necessity of making this the object of a pompous "training session."

That evening, I met up with Laurent Folliot in the basement cafeteria, which has greatly changed since then, but which, if I'm not mistaken, still exists. At the entrance, there were some public-access computers. We sat side by side, each taking possession of a machine; we set our beers down beside the keyboards. That's where, at a distance of one meter, we exchanged our first emails. Seeing as we could speak in person, these were completely devoid of content, unfit to deliver anything but their own nature—"this is an email," "so is this"—a simultaneously ironic and perfect, albeit probably unfair, illustration of Marshall McLuhan's maxim from the 1960s, when he prophesied that from now on the *medium* is the message. I only have a very dim and perhaps false memory of the moment, and unfortunately when my account was terminated I didn't see fit to archive any of these very first emails—so I can't say whether we made this joke at the end of our brief exchange, the interest of which rapidly faded, as you can imagine. Then we went back and slumped into the cafeteria's old torn armchairs, without having glimpsed the future immensity of the things with which we had just played.

•

The other day, as I was walking on rue du Temple, an image flashed through my mind of what life was like before the internet. It was a room with books covering the walls and a telephone at the foot of the bed. I was using this telephone to call Guy-Cédric Werlings, and, while compulsively thumbing through the volumes of our respective libraries, we were asking each other for hours on end: "Do you remember in which of Plato's dialogues Socrates says...."; "Could you find me the paragraph of Spinoza's *Ethics* where he gives the example of....."; etc.

•

Among the phenomena that belonged to this past world and will soon disappear are the drawings we used to scribble with one hand while talking on the telephone. Our other hand held the receiver, but we could wedge it against our shoulder by tilting our head when we needed both hands, to hold down the piece of paper on which our pencil ran. These "telephone doodles" were a product of the immobility that home phones imposed on us; we almost never make them anymore—there are so many other things we can do while talking to people on the phone. We barely even noticed they had ceased to exist. We lost them before we had the chance to collect them, study them, exhibit them, perhaps, in galleries or museums. I remember my father used to leave remarkable ones, on the little round table that proudly enthroned the house's only telephone.

•

One winter morning, I awoke with the memory of this dream: beyond the shore of the little resort town in Brittany where I was staying for a few days, I could see large white swans passing, amid sparkling reflections of sun and ocean. The image was brief and dazzling. What troubled me, upon waking, wasn't the hidden meaning the scene might possibly contain; it was that my first reflex, within the dream, had been to photograph these swans with my smartphone and tell myself: I absolutely have to post this on Facebook. Was I going to become one of those people who constantly ask themselves whether the experience they are having would make a good Facebook "status update"? And why not, after all? This might be our new ethics. Who am I to struggle against the tide. And I stopped thinking about it.

A few days later, finding myself near La Forêt-Fouesnant, I decided to go see the ria that we often used to visit when I was a child, and which I liked very much, because the path that ran alongside it led over a little footbridge to the Port-la-Forêt marina, where there were always many sailboats to watch. The last time I had been there was in August 2003. With a few friends, I had ferried a boat from La Corogne, and we had landed in this port after a week of cold, damp sailing in the Bay of Biscay. That evening, beside this path on which I hadn't set foot in more than ten years, we found a crêperie where we had dinner. France was in the midst of a heat wave, but we hadn't had any inkling of it.

As these different layers of memory heaved in my mind, I glimpsed an almost empty parking lot where I could leave my car, next to the mudflats. When I had put an end to the to-and-fro of the windshield wipers, I saw a flock of majestic swans peacefully gliding along the shallow water that remained at low tide, and I had the feeling of remembering—with some uncertainty—that it wasn't rare to see them in this place when I was a child.

Back in Paris, I posted this story as a status update on Facebook.

•

A. and I were in an art-house movie theater in the Latin Quarter. As we entered the hall, I had the feeling we had already been there not so long ago. Nevertheless, I was completely unable to identify when, or to see what film; and I was troubled by the irresolvable contradiction between my feeling, which caused me to place this moment in the very recent past, perhaps ten days or a few weeks ago at the most, and the material certainty that it must have been longer than that—but I was incapable of placing this "longer than that" into any definite time frame. I put the question to A., and, to pin down my memory while at the same time helping her revive her own (which I was keen to do, for I was beginning to wonder whether I hadn't fallen prey to a particularly hallucinatory and slightly worrisome case of déjà vu), I added that we had said to each other, on that day, as we entered the hall exactly as we were doing now, that it had been a very long while since we had last been to the cinema. This indeed sounded familiar to her. The farther we advanced down the central aisle, the more we both remembered having been there and having chosen more or less the same seats, on the right, near the screen, and having told ourselves it had been months or years since we had last been to the movies (though she and I had often visited this very cinema, Le Champollion, before we knew each other, and later we had often gone together). But A. thought it was in September, that is, more than six months earlier, which I found hard to believe. The room went dark; the film started. It was Bertolucci's *Before the Revolution*. Plunged into darkness, facing a stream of images I couldn't fully concentrate on, I tried in vain to grope my

way toward a few scattered scraps of memory out of which to reconstruct the scene missing from my past.

I asked myself what digital trace our visit might have left, and
I couldn't think of any. No doubt we had decided to go to the cinema
without needing to mark the occasion with a text message or, still
less, an email. At the ticket booth, debit cards weren't accepted. Bank
statements would therefore be of no help in resolving the enigma,
despite their power of recollection, which had first struck me ten
years earlier—a completely obvious power as soon as you think
about and experience it, although a very understandable inner reluc-
tance initially keeps us from according the least poetry to such an
object. Could one find the program archives of the various Latin
Quarter cinemas online? Very unlikely. Would I have to rely on the
chance that a ticket might have been left in a jacket or coat pocket,
a ticket I might find again later—if I hadn't thrown it away—after
a few days or a few months, as can happen when the season is changing and the ticket remains in the pocket of a piece of clothing one
doesn't wear again for a long time. I felt as though I were floundering
in the depths of a sea of oblivion.

In the middle of the film, a scene set off a vague but effective
association of ideas that suddenly seemed to answer my question
and calm the troubles my memory was giving me. When we were
leaving, I said to A., confidently, "In fact, the film we saw here not
so long ago was Losey's *Accident*." But she rejected this hypothesis
with even stauncher certitude than my own: we had seen *Accident*
at L'Action Écoles. My hypothesis, which I now had to resign myself
to abandon, had aligned very well with my feeling of temporal prox-
imity, and I was at an even greater loss to see what I could replace it

with. As we walked in the night and spoke of other things, this question still echoed in a corner of my mind. I was beginning to lose all hope of finding an answer. We sure aren't *googleable*, I said to myself. The last questions that remain unanswerable are those related to the events of our lives. The sensation of this incapacity struck me as something new. Had the widespread use of Google weakened our faculty of memory, as the decline of a function provokes the atrophy of an organ? Or had the contrast between the internet and ourselves suddenly brought to light an imperfection we formerly had no reason to lament bitterly or even particularly to notice?

Just before we crossed the Seine, facing Notre Dame, I remembered that the film we had gone to see at the Champollion a few weeks earlier was Albert Lewin's *Pandora*. This recollection caught me by surprise; nothing had summoned it. The strange astonishment I felt at this absolutely spontaneous surfacing of the past—without having pressed a single key or pieced together the slightest association of ideas—seemed new to me as well.

•

I had, in a certain sense, forgotten I had a memory. Faced with this mental "blank," I had sought the help of a digital auxiliary that in turn had come up short. Plato's prophecy in the myth of Theuth was suddenly made concrete, on a vaster scale. Theuth, as Socrates recounts in *Phaedrus*, had invented writing and presented it to the king of Egypt with the explanation that this invention would resolve the failures of human memory; but the king had replied that this remedy would be no remedy at all. Those who used it would cease to exercise their memory and their souls would become forgetful; they would commit things to memory externally and not internally. With the internet—which fulfills to a supreme degree the externalization of memory first initiated by writing—we might get the feeling that we have simultaneously become capable of forgetting nothing and incapable of remembering anything at all.

•

In the past, we would sometimes forget stanzas of a poem, historical facts, theorems, Latin words, etc., things we had learned in school because previous generations had deemed them essential   or even things we had learned for pleasure, out of a sense of vocation, but which still threatened to escape us if we didn't make an effort to retain them. Our memory of external things seemed vulnerable and dependent upon our will; our personal memory, however, was like a fortress. From time to time, we might forget who was prime minister in 1952, or who won the World Cup in 1970, but we could assure ourselves that at least there was one thing we'd never forget, or that— barring some tragic accident—we'd never forget as entirely as all of the rest, and that was our own life.

Now that the internet has equipped us with a gigantic auxiliary memory capable of making up for just about every lapse in our recollection of external facts, it is rather our personal memory that suddenly, by this new contrast, seems afflicted with a disquieting imprecision. My life, our lives, are unverifiable, while more and more things are verifiable on Google—things we would formerly have believed forever lost to memory. If I have a question about how the Battle of Leuctra was fought, the internet replies; if I have a question about a moment in my past, it doesn't reply. I had a daydream that one day we would find on the internet the traces of even the most insignificant events of our existence, those that don't have any chance of being cataloged by anyone, as if everything that took place automatically recorded itself and the internet was simply the medium that gave access to Being's spontaneous memory of itself. If this were possible, we would have the feeling of entering into a hitherto unknown dimension. But the fact that it isn't possible also creates a strangeness, perhaps no less intense. What most intimately concerns us is now among the most uncertain things of this world—the things least susceptible to being reassuringly verified. The borders of our own identity are becoming blurred, while objects everywhere are gaining distinct, firmly established biographies. We haven't changed, but the things around us have changed, and we have fallen into the category of fragile beings in a kind of ontological backwater, like an old neighborhood in a vastly expanding city, a neighborhood increasingly lost amid ever more numerous, more modern, more solid buildings, looking down at us from on high.

•

But perhaps we will get our revenge. It is likely that this fragility of personal memory is limited to those amphibious beings who have lived a significant portion of their lives before the advent of the internet. I'm thirty-seven years old; I went online for the first time when I was nineteen; I can still say I've lived more than half my life without the internet, though this ratio will soon tip the other way. Perhaps those who grow up with the internet will leave enough traces of themselves to find their way through their own memories without fail. Their personal cartography will have lost its unknown territories. They will no longer bury their secrets in nothingness; they will bury them in the infinite.

Maël Renouard, born in Paris in 1979, is a novelist, essayist, and translator. He has taught philosophy at the Sorbonne and the École Normale Supérieure on the rue d'Ulm, of which he is a graduate. Between 2009 and 2012, he worked as a speechwriter for the prime minister of France. His novella *La Réforme de l'opéra de Pékin* (The Reform of the Peking Opera) received the Prix Décembre in 2013, and his novel *L'Historiographe du royaume* (The Historiographer of the Kingdom) was named a finalist for the 2020 Prix Goncourt.

Peter Behrman de Sinéty grew up in Maine and teaches English at the École Normale Supérieure in Paris.